Twilight of the American Experiment

Without Moral Balance, Our Republic Will Fall

Twilight of the American Experiment

Without Moral Balance, Our Republic Will Fall

Michael C. Anderson

SBPC

Simms Books Publishing Corporation

SBPC

SIMMS BOOKS PUBLISHING CORP.

Publishers Since 2012

Published By Simms Books Publishing

Jonesboro, GA

2023916467

Library of Congress Cataloging in Publication Data

Michael C. Anderson

Twilight of the American Experiment

Without Moral Balance, Our Republic Will Fall

ISBN: 978-1-949433-51-7

Printed in the United States of America

Editor: Monica Lamb

Cover by: Michael C. Anderson

Dedication

For Shelly and Eric Anderson

Acknowledgment

I wish to thank Monica Lamb for helping out with the edits.

Table of Contents

Dedication I

Acknowledgment II

Preface IV

1 Introduction 1

2 Polymorphism and The Genetic Variance in Morality 11

3 Biological Conservatism Before the Enlightenment 19

4 Liberal Thinking Emerges During the Enlightenment 29

5 The Welfare State 51

6 Socialist Ideology Matures 65

7 Academia Moves to the Left 85

8 Mainstream Media Moves to the Left 103

9 Social Media Leans Left 119

10 Woke Corporations 135

11 The Eroding of American Traditions 143

12 The Failure of Conservatism 161

13 Why Moral Balance Matters 175

14 Can The American Experiment Survive? 191

Bibliography 213

PREFACE

As a historian and student of political systems, I study today's political currents, identifying links to the past that help us understand today's politics. History is a guide, not a predictor, because human society adapts to competing political forces as they exist during a specific period. Every age and situation is unique. Still, we can put history to good use.

As I started thinking about my fourth book, I had my mind on 2020 and the events at the end of the Trump presidency. The first impeachment of Trump began in December 2019. Then, the beginning of 2020 saw the left continuing attacks on Trump, trying to discredit him and improve their chances of defeating him in the November election. That distraction masked the onset of the COVID pandemic in the United States, which smoldered through February.

By early March, the pandemic was underway, and that month saw America move into shutdown mode. By May, the country began to open, but the economy's return was eclipsed by protests and riots related to the George Floyd murder. COVID returned in late summer, and lockdowns closed most schools, so students were taught online.

The pandemic created a chance for America to unite and fight the disease, but that didn't happen. When a formidable outside agency threatened the United States in every previous instance, the country joined and won the battle.

This time, the two-decade-long tribal divide sabotaged the government's management of the pandemic and unleashed political warfare.

Trump was attacked for his response to the COVID virus. He made a few missteps but pushed the vaccine research forward very quickly. Many therapies were attempted to slow the spread of the virus because nothing was known about its behavior. Most did not work. The CDC was unprepared for a pandemic, so ramping up its processes took significant time. Even then, it showed itself to be an inefficient bureaucracy. Too many elderly and compromised patients died because they weren't protected.

After the initial lockdown phase in the spring of 2020, blue and red states adopted different strategies to fight the disease. Blue states were more aggressive about lockdowns. Red states were lenient, believing that aggressive lockdowns damaged the economy and disrupted society. The first vaccines were delivered in December 2020, after Trump was defeated. With Biden's election, the COVID narrative flipped from a Republican strategy to a Democrat one, emphasizing lockdowns as necessary to end the pandemic. Biden pushed the blue state lockdown strategy as a national plan as he and the Democratic Party moved to the left and began implementing a radical progressive agenda.

Biden surprised many in both political parties when he adopted the progressive ideology. Most voters expected him to be consistent with his decades-long track record of moderation, but the American people were fooled.

Over the past few decades, the left has expanded its control over American society through academia, the media, and the evolving social culture. This one-sided power grab has the potential to destroy our nation. The federal government is operating far left of the political center and counter to the political beliefs of more than half of the county. The path taken by Biden has raised the level of tribalism in America and reduced the likelihood that progress will be made in solving the many problems America faces.

Our political system requires consensus between different points of view to move forward. Without compromise, it will remain stalled, and our society will wither.

A biological term, polymorphism, is at the center of the discussion in this book. Polymorphism is an evolutionary adaptation characterized by genes that can be expressed in different forms. For example, human eye color is a typical example of polymorphism at work.

Polymorphism exists in human personality traits and informs our views about morality. More specifically, human moral foundations are heritable and influenced by the environment during a child's development. They produce a spectrum of behaviors that give humans different world views. Evolution created this variation to allow humans to adapt to rapid changes in their ecosystem and increase their chances of survival. Nowadays, that variation matters because those at opposite ends of the political spectrum have views unacceptable to the other side.

The left believes it knows how a society should move forward. The right has a different view. Until recently, the views of the left and right competed to control the direction of American society. But now, the left dominance of academia, the media, and the cultural narrative have allowed them to dominate the communication of ideas in America. The left's cancel culture mentality stifles dissent and dialogue, so anyone representing a point of view outside of left dogma is ridiculed and demeaned.

This book will identify, describe, and characterize the left's takeover of American society. It has been 50 years in the making, and the right has been unsuccessful in opposing this development. The right is indifferent to politics and does not put forth the effort needed to counter the left. Lack of action on their part forfeits the chance to stabilize the American culture narrative.

Two factors can save the country: More aggressive opposition from conservatives and greater engagement on the part of traditional liberals, moderates, and independent voters to counter the ideology being pursued by the left. Independents resist ideas far from the center, which makes them immune from the lure of ideology. That's why they must recognize and act on their critical role of moderating extreme views.

CHAPTER ONE

INTRODUCTION

The two-hundred-year American political experiment is under attack by those who wish to replace it with a new system. The supporters of this vision, socialists of many types, suggest their ideology will make America a better place. They imagine a world of equality that guarantees equal opportunity and outcomes for all Americans. That world would eliminate poverty and homelessness, provide free education, good jobs for all, and build a multicultural society living in peace and happiness. To achieve that vision, America must discard its founding principles, political system, and current way of life.

The recipe for this new way of life is socialist ideology, a set of ideas that has universally failed in every implementation throughout history. One might ask how a failed ideology can replace a system that stands as a model for the world. Advocates of socialism say it failed, in the past, because its implementations were faulty. Those who understand history, however, can see that socialism is an ideological model designed to create a utopian world that's impossible to

1

achieve. Despite this reality, socialists remain amazingly stubborn and never give up.

Socialist thinking evolved from the moral ideology of the political left, which has always possessed an uncompromising desire to create a world of human equality. That narrowly-focused morality, partly genetic, puts caring and fairness above other human moral foundations such as respect for authority, loyalty, and sanctity. The right does not share the left's passion for equality because it believes a hierarchy, the natural human social structure, should be maintained in any political system.

The philosopher Jean Jacques Rousseau (1712-1778) introduced the first collectivist ideas, which helped define a socialist world. Since Rousseau's time, there has been an open debate between collectivists and Enlightenment thinkers who believe the individual must be the focal point of human society. Rousseau believed the proper role of government was to address the needs of groups rather than individuals.

For most of American history, collectivism was no more than an interesting idea, attempted elsewhere as socialist model implementations. The American people chose the Enlightenment values of Western civilization as the foundation for the American culture because they saw those values as a roadmap to freedom. Collectivist ideas were never part of the design of the American political system.

American Liberalism

At the turn of the 20th Century, the Progressive Movement, at its core a collectivist concept, significantly contributed to correcting government corruption and unfair treatment of workers. History records those progressive efforts as invaluable in improving the lives of all Americans. Later, the poverty and want of the Great Depression drove the creation of an American welfare state designed to create programs that provided a safety net for all Americans.

During the Depression, socialism became a popular alternative to capitalism, and the country took sides over which system offered more significant opportunities. Roosevelt opted for the capitalists because he needed them to implement his welfare state programs. Progressives fell out of favor after World War II ended because of their close relationship with world communists. As the Cold War unfolded, anyone associated with communists was considered a traitor to America.

The Vietnam War drove an entire generation to react against the establishment, rejecting American politics and culture in the name of change. The 1960s began a cultural takeover by the left, and by the early 2000s, that takeover had encompassed academia, the mainstream media, America's cultural dialogue, and the new social media platforms.

The Enlightenment Expression in America

Before the Enlightenment, individuals, who lacked wealth and influence, were ignored by their government. After the Enlightenment, the ordinary people, as individuals, had secured the rights and the freedoms needed to pursue a better life. As a part of the capitalist economy, they could earn money by working at a job or starting their own business. Technology was the engine that facilitated human efficiency and pushed society forward more quickly. Democracies emerged, giving most citizens the power to vote and hold elected officials accountable.

American Traditions

From its beginning, America has demonstrated a character unlike other nations. The idealistic people who founded this nation escaped the oppression of Western Europe and came with the hope of settling a vast continent with unlimited opportunity and building a political system using Enlightenment values. After the Constitution was created in 1787, the United States began to operate a political system, allowing people to control their lives without government intrusion.

Conservative Views

A conservative mindset has always been a part of the American fabric. Americans have stood for family, community, and religious traditions. They welcomed the freedom of a new age but wanted to ensure their government supported the traditions they cherished most.

Conservatism had no political voice in American politics until 1854 when the Republican Party was created to take a political stand against slavery. Abraham Lincoln, the new party's most important representative, led the country through the Civil War, the most challenging in American history. Lincoln's leadership enabled the party to guide America into the post-Civil War period, even without him. Most Americans supported the Republican Party from the post-Civil War period until the early 20th Century when the Progressive Movement migrated from the Republican to the Democratic Party.

After the stock market crash in 1929, Republicans were forced to take a back seat to New Deal programs. The American Liberalism model of Franklin D. Roosevelt (1882-1945) survived until the 1970s when it failed due to wasteful and ineffective government welfare programs. As the liberal model faded, the Republican Party emerged as an ideologically-driven party for the first time. The ideas of William F. Buckley (1925-2008) and others built a common conservative ideology around traditions, capitalism, and anti-communism. Republican success faded as the New-Left progressives became more potent in the 1970s and 1980s.

Conservatives see the last 30 years of political change as dangerous. They can live with the changing culture but will not tolerate an attack on America's traditions and values. They see the left as trying to create a future removed from beliefs that propelled the Enlightenment forward.

Tribalism at Work

Efforts on the part of the left to redefine the American political system have accelerated tribalism, and now a chasm divides Americans based on party affiliation. The political and ideological center is gone because its torchbearers retired in the 1990s, leaving the government to ideologues in both parties far from the center. There is no mention of compromise and bi-partisan cooperation because each side believes the other is misguided and dangerous.

As we move into 2023, the tribes remain locked in their views. The left is focused on identity politics, socialist programs, global warming, and the remnants of COVID. The right is focused on beating back the attack on American history and traditions while fighting the country's money-wasting journey toward a welfare state. How this battle plays out will determine the future of the American political system.

Why Moral Balance Matters

The imbalance in America's political morality is potentially catastrophic for its future. Without moral balance, there can be no agreement on the programs and policies needed to move the country forward.

Variation in human political morality was a product of evolution.[1] A million years ago, when primitive humans began encountering new ecosystems, they needed a mechanism to adapt to different environments. Evolution provided the adaptive behaviors that improved human survivability.

---

[1] Tim Dean. *Evolution and Moral Diversity*. Morality and the Cognitive Sciences, Volume 7 October, 2012, p. 116

Behavioral flexibility came about as a product of a genetic characteristic called polymorphism. Polymorphic genes express themselves in multiple forms, and challenges in an animal's environment determine the expression of polymorphism. Moths evolve to adapt their color to their surroundings, so they become disguised. That adaptation develops because camouflaged moths survive, and those who are easy to see do not. Camouflaged moths become more frequent in their environment, and the trait is strengthened.

In human beings, our personality traits, including our moral foundations, are attributable to polymorphism. In the primitive world, humans lived nomadic lives searching for food. As man encountered different ecosystems, each required specific behavioral traits to maximize the opportunity for obtaining and maintaining a food supply. Polymorphism modified human behavioral traits to create two basic preferences: the desire to explore and manage the food supply. The explorers were better adapted to a food-poor environment requiring constant searching. The managers were better adapted for controlling food-rich settings that did not require exploration. There were no politics in the primitive world, so those adaptations increased human survivability through decision-making by consensus.

During the Enlightenment period, those traits developed into political behavior. Those hunters from the past became liberals because they desired change and were open to new experiences. Those managers from the past became

7

conservatives because they were cautious and preferred the status quo. What would have happened if only one of these groups existed? Liberals would always be trying new things and taking too many risks. Conservatives would never try new things and miss opportunities to improve the likelihood of their survival.

These variations in political morality require consensus to work. Both liberals and conservatives must be open to the opinions of the other group. With an agreement, the American political system can work. Each side controls a portion of the legislative branch. Neither side has a filibuster-proof majority, so the parties must work together.

Outside government, there is a more significant imbalance between the left and right because the left has taken control of public communication in the United States. This control extends to higher education, K-12 education, mainstream media, social media, and the American cultural narrative.

Format of This Book
Chapter 1: *Introduction* and background for the topics discussed in the book.

Chapter 2: *Polymorphism and the Genetic Variance in Morality,* describes how genetic polymorphism relates to human morality. Through natural selection, human moral foundations are variable across the population. That variation has existed as long as humans have walked the earth.

Chapter 3: *Biological Conservatism Before the Enlightenment* describes how conservatives-controlled pre-Enlightenment societies. Their focus on power, loyalty, and authority was better suited to the structure of those societies.

Chapter 4: *Biological Liberalism* emerged during the Enlightenment. This chapter discusses how liberal thinking emerged from the Enlightenment. In America, social justice beliefs stimulated liberals to develop political models that expanded equality.

Chapter 5: *The Welfare State* traces the first implementation of large government social programs.

Chapter 6: *Socialist Ideology After Rousseau* covers the history of socialism after Rousseau, including its many attempts to produce a workable model.

Chapter 7: *Academia Moves Left* describes when American academia moved hard left and began pushing a left ideology into the public arena. In the 21st Century, academia has adopted censorship to silence the right.

Chapter 8: *Mainstream Media Moves Left* presents the growing partisanship of the mainstream media along with its censoring of the Right.

Chapter 9: *Social Media on the Left* describes how Big Tech companies have joined academia and the mainstream media in a concerted effort to block conservative ideas from the public.

9

Chapter 10: *Woke Corporations* describes how America's large corporations have absorbed radical left ideas into their business models and image. The corporations explicitly did this to benefit their businesses. They understand money can be made by adopting woke behavior, and they use their new model to cover up past and current misbehavior.

Chapter 11: *The Eroding of America's Traditions* describes the overt effort of the left to attack and do away with American traditions. The Left hopes that success in this endeavor will pave the way for socialism.

Chapter 12: *The Failure of Conservatism,* describes how the psychology of conservatives compromises their ability to fight the left for control of the American cultural narrative.

Chapter 13: *Why Moral Balance Matters,* lays out why a balance in American political morality is essential for the stability and well-being of our republic.

Chapter 14: *Can the American Experiment Survive*? This chapter discusses what's ahead for the United States if our political morality can't be rebalanced.

CHAPTER TWO

POLYMORPHISM AND THE GENETIC VARIANCE IN MORALITY

To neglect the common ground with other primates, and to deny the evolutionary roots of human morality, would be like arriving at the top of a tower to declare that the rest of the building is irrelevant, that the precious concept of "tower" ought to be reserved for the summit. **Frans de Waal**

To anyone paying attention, it is evident that there is a wide variation in American political views. Observe what tribal America has become over the last twenty years and the range of opinions and emotions that flow from it. These variations were not caused by misunderstandings or avoiding the truth. They came from genetic and environmental factors that influence the development of human political morality. Before the current tribal period, both sides of the political spectrum were willing to work together to solve problems affecting our country. Still, changes in American culture have eroded the middle ground, previously a wellspring for consensus. Without a middle ground, only the extremes remain.

This chapter describes the genetic and environmental forces that produce variations in human political morality. These distinctions include behavioral adaptations designed to provide an evolutionary benefit and increase the odds of human survival.

Human Development

Human beings became the dominant species because of their large, capable brain. Humans can eat various foods as omnivores and survive in different environments. Humans are social animals more comfortable living with others than living in solitude. Because of this preference for social living, humans faced the problem of living successfully in groups that included unrelated individuals.

Early on, human bands comprised kinship groups, with multiple families joined by related paternity. Eventually, groups became more extensive and began to include non-blood-related individuals. The inclusion of strangers dictated caution because the stranger's motives were uncertain.

Humans adapted their behavior to mitigate the risk of working with outsiders.[2] Their cheater detection mechanism and the use of gossip are two examples of this adaptation. The cheater detection mechanism is a brain function that monitors information to validate the legitimacy of a transaction between individuals. These transactions must have a conditional element that needs to be satisfied. For

---

[2] Robert Axelrod and William D. Hamilton. The Evolution of Cooperation. Science, New Series, Vol. 211, No. 4489 (Mar. 27, 1981), pp. 1390-1396

example, I give my friend a tool expecting him to do something for me in return. My cheater mechanism will remember whether that person has met his obligation. Gossip has a similar function. Asking others whether an individual is trustworthy helps a person validate the value of a relationship with that person.

As we observe other human beings, we notice apparent physical differences. Some people are large, some small, some wide, and some narrow. Beneath the surface, we cannot see differences, particularly in our brains, which showcase the most significant variation between us. No two human brains are alike.

Among other functions, the brain houses our personality, the behavioral traits determining how we function in the world, by ourselves, and in contact with others. One aspect of personality is morality, which dictates how we must work as a group member. These rules might include "do not harm someone unless they try to harm you" or "don't trust someone you don't know." Before agriculture, human morality was uncomplicated because human beings lived in small groups. The advent of agriculture and its ability to facilitate a more significant population density required a new kind of morality called political morality. This term describes how personal moral views operate in a complex human society. For example, one person might say that society has to be more equitable. Another person may say the opposite. Why the difference?

Why don't all human beings wish for the same kind of society?

That difference is due to a variation in political morality across a population. Some are on the left, some are on the right, and some are in the middle. The spectrum of political morality is genetic, an inherited behavior developed as an environmental adaptation.

In the primitive world, human migrations introduced new heterogeneous environments with varying climates and food supplies. Humans had to adapt to these environments to survive. Natural selection took too long to produce the required changes, so a different type of adaptation was used, one that could produce more rapid change. Polymorphism is an evolutionary action that produces rapid transformation by creating a spectrum of behaviors. In operation, it creates two or more different forms in a species using one gene or group of genes. Its typical function is maintaining various forms in a population living in heterogeneous environments. The most obvious example is sexual dimorphism, referring to differences between the sexes within a species. In human beings, we see it in the difference in size between men and women.

In the primitive world, polymorphism created adaptations that enhanced man's efforts to manage food supplies in a changing environment. It created one group that aggressively sought change, who would hunt when food supplies were low. It also created another group, the food managers, who were organized and well-suited to manage the food supply when food was abundant. In the small group setting of the primitive world, members with these different viewpoints were brought together to make decisions by consensus. When no agreement could be reached, leaders made the decisions.

The polymorphic adaptation is dynamic and does not reduce itself to a single stable state. In the spectrum, the adaptations work against each other, change frequency, and adapt to the environment. Frequency-dependent selection uses environmental feedback to prioritize different behavior versions to maintain flexibility. In the case of the food-finding adaptation, the spectrum is maintained by a negative frequency-dependent process. In other words, if there are more hunters than food managers in a group, the adaptation will increase the number of food managers to maintain the balance across the spectrum. The adaptation is driven by decreasing numbers in one group rather than increasing numbers in the other group. Polymorphism has limits and cannot produce an infinite number of variations. Therefore, working together, a series of genes are responsible for the adaptation. That group of genes creates variation in the way humans view the world.

People are forced to make moral judgments all the time. Often the decisions are not easy. Having a mix of moral positions within a group allows for dialogue and debate over the options so the best decisions can be made.

The advent of agriculture and animal husbandry changed the dynamics of human social interactions forever because it supported large populations in a small space.[3] People used to a small group, where all members were known, were now exposed to many strangers. Large social groups required a structure to allocate limited resources, such as food, and provide civil control over human behavior, so governments emerged to act in that role. Consensus decision-making disappeared with the advent of social hierarchies because the government created and enforced political morality. That political morality consisted of whatever those in power said it should include. Individuals had no input unless they had power, so most were limited to praising or complaining about the government. The top of the hierarchy received more resources and benefits than the others, leaving little for the lower classes. Hierarchical societies create winners and losers in their communities, but social hierarchies have remained pervasive across human cultures throughout history. They occur naturally in all social groups because they promote productivity.

Before the Enlightenment, human society focused on the group: religious groups, social class groups, and economic class groups. Government action was directed toward group needs and group demands. The Enlightenment changed that focus from group to individual, recognizing that the individual human being had a value separate from the group he belonged to. The individual would become the engine of

---

[3] Harner, Michael J. *Population Pressure and the Social Evolution of Agriculturalists.* Southwestern Journal of Anthropology, Spring, 1970, Vol. 26, No. 1, pp. 67-86.

the post-Enlightenment period via his power over government action.

The individual could now demand the right to vote in elections and be protected from government intrusion by a constitution and bill of rights. People began to notice that others shared their political morality, so groups with the same views organized to increase their influence. The primitive moral spectrum of hunters and managers, who had helped the early man find and manage his food supply, saw their former identities reemerge during this period. The hunters still wanted change, so they became liberals (or anti-conservatives). Their goal was to change human society into something better. The old food managers became conservatives favoring traditions and the status quo. The first politicians appeared to represent these ideologies, vying for political office. Eventually, they came to represent political parties created to coordinate the choosing of candidates for elections.

There were no formal political parties in the United States immediately after the Constitution was enacted. Factionalism was in play because of fundamental disagreements about the division of power between the states and the federal government. The Federalist faction, led by Alexander Hamilton, wanted a strong centralized government, while Democratic-Republicans, represented by Thomas Jefferson, wanted the states to share government power. The Federalists were the conservatives seeking to maintain a traditional centralized government. The Democratic-Republicans were the liberals seeking a partner relationship between the states and the federal government. In the 1796 election, John Adams narrowly defeated Thomas Jefferson. Adams ran as a member of the Federalist Party. When Jefferson beat Adams in 1800, the Federalist Party fell out of power and would never win another election. They fielded candidates until 1816, but there was little opposition to the Democrat-Republicans until 1828 when Andrew Jackson renamed Jefferson's party the Democratic Party.

During the Jacksonian era, the Whig Party became the conservative opposition. The Whigs eventually became the Republican Party.

Throughout American history, liberals and conservatives have fought for control of the American government, hunters against food managers.

Today, the divide between left and right has the most significant impact in the country's history. The left has never pushed such an extremist agenda on the American people, an agenda that ruthlessly attacks conservatives and conservative traditions. The right, in defense of its views, strengthened its tribal opposition. There is no consensus about moving America forward. There is no leader to decide which tribe is right.

Americans need to consider their connections to the other tribe and how that connection was instrumental to their survival. Hunters cooperated with managers. Both understood the value of different points of view. Both accepted consensus as the best way to make the right decision.

CHAPTER THREE

BIOLOGICAL CONSERVATISM BEFORE THE ENLIGHTENMENT

I've always believed that conservatism is the politics of reality, and that reality ultimately asserts itself in a reasonably free society, in behalf of the conservative position. **William F. Buckley, Jr.**

Human social behavior evolved due to the advanced intelligence of human beings, which included the evolutionary adaptations needed to function efficiently in social settings. Humans prefer social relationships rather than being alone. Families needed protection, which required building relationships with those outside the family. The question of why humans adopt altruistic behavior without knowing whether they would receive something else in return answers itself. Altruistic behavior formed the basis for relationship building.

The Primitive World

For most of their time on earth, humans have lived in small, nomadic groups that moved from place to place in search of food. Human evolutionary morality made them conservative and cautious or liberal and adventurous. The conservative and cautious morality was prompted by the desire to manage an abundant food supply. The liberal and adventurous morality was stimulated by a desire to hunt for food.

Consider the following example showing how these different views worked together. A group of tribesmen decided they wanted to go hunting for meat. In this case, one or two wild pigs might feed the tribe. The previous day, a scout had observed a herd of pigs nearby. That scout also watched a few lions in the area. The hunters discussed among themselves how to conduct the hunt. Those we call liberals were eager to begin and looked forward to it. They saw the hunt as an opportunity to earn recognition by securing an ample food supply. The conservatives were more circumspect and worried about the lions. They remembered a recent hunt in which three of their fellow tribes-people were killed without warning when lions suddenly appeared. They suggested scouts observe the herd for a day or two longer to see if the lions remained in the area. The liberals didn't like that idea; they felt it was overly cautious and a waste of time.

Liberals might have viewed the scouting report as benign, while conservatives viewed the same information as threatening. A decision based on consideration of these views was necessary to move forward. Tribal leaders decided in favor of the liberals, so the hunt went on.

Without a mix of opinions, any group of liberals would be wiped out quickly due to faulty and dangerous risk-taking.

Any group of conservatives would avoid risk in situations that warranted action, resulting in stifled progress.

Biological Conservatives and Advanced Human Society

The Neolithic period (circa 10,000 BCE) saw rapid changes in human social structure as groups began to implement agriculture and the domestication of animals. The ability of one individual to influence a group's direction was now limited because his group was much more significant. Activities impacting the individual were now determined by a hierarchical, leadership-based government structure that operated outside the individual's personal and familial space.

The psychological balance between a liberal change agent and the conservative status quo no longer worked under this new social structure. Those in power projected a political morality on the rest of the population. Individuals, who disagreed with the direction of the government, had no say unless they held enough power to influence the leaders.

Conservatives occupied a position of dominance in human society from the time of the first governments until the Enlightenment Period began in 1650 CE. Conservative access to power was based on the connection between conservative political morality and the hierarchical structure of governments. Leaders demanded loyalty and respect for their authority, characteristics ingrained in the conservative's morality.

21

Liberals were less likely to obtain positions of power in the ancient world because those positions did not allow them to act on their moral beliefs. Liberal moral psychology was focused on caring and fairness, which drove them to seek equality, but equality had no advocates in the power centers of the ancient world.

Conservative leaders expected loyalty among their followers, and those followers sanctioned their leader's authority through their support. Those leaders used traditions as a tool for legitimacy, consistent with a conservative view of the world. Respect for authority was a part of living in an authoritarian society; leaders constantly tried to remind the people of their power.

Greek Conservatism and Authority
The Greeks created the notion of progress because they were the first to conceptualize and implement new ideas. As they saw it, progress came from using creativity to acquire knowledge. Wisdom came from knowledge obtained from observing the world.

Aristotle (384-322 BCE) believed morality and politics, unlike natural science, lacked experts, so human experience over generations was the primary source of morality. Greek conservatism enhanced a cultural belief in a glorious past and natural order. As innovative as the Greeks were, their traditionalism had to adapt to change, as seen in their constantly changing democracy. Greek conservatism was about preserving the natural way. Using a democratic process to achieve these ideals was not only possible but the most effective path forward. The ability to balance new and old implied that Greek conservatism was more than a political ideology. If it had been, the Greeks would not have tolerated conflicting political beliefs. Traditionalism was a collective belief in the Greek way of life.

Greek philosophers embraced nationalism, though there was neither a single Greek nation nor a common Hellenic type. They were surprisingly devoted to tradition, given their affinity for what was new. They were intolerant of repression yet considered dissent regarding philosophical teachings inappropriate. They were conservative about writing, preferring the spoken word. The Greeks were enamored with the legends of their ancestors, passed down by oral tradition.

Following the death of Alexander (356-323 BCE), the city-state declined as the Greeks moved toward an individualism that made humans more conscious of themselves, more impatient with the regulations of society, and made their literature more individualistic. This new philosophical view was foreign to the Greek tradition and focused on the whole society. The sophists arose as teachers and orators who believed the individual should be the center of society because only the individual could control his own life. Sophists did not win their debates with logic; they won by making the best impression. Greek individualism foreshadowed the same phenomenon that would emerge during the Enlightenment Period.

Roman Conservatism

The Romans were opposites to the Greeks in thought and action. Practical people focused on their agrarian world; the Romans were not interested in taking time for philosophical thought. They were builders interested in creating the structures needed to make life easier as opposed to the idle pondering of theoretical ideas. The Roman political system was an experiment in building a society. Its government began as a monarchy, but eventually, the king was overthrown by the wealthy class who created the republic.

For the first two centuries of the Roman Republic, conservatives were in control. The patrician class controlled the Senate, which acted in its interest, ignoring the rights of the plebeians. A strict two-class system existed, dividing the rich and the poor. Loyalty to family and country was endemic to Roman thinking. Authority was the basis for the Roman government, and trust was placed in wise men to make critical decisions.

Over time, Roman society changed as a new middle class appeared. The knights emerged as a class that accumulated wealth through hard work and used that wealth to demand political influence. They sought to rise out of their position in the plebeian class by agitating for more rights, and the Senate granted those rights slowly over time.

As plebeians gained rights, they demanded the opportunity to hold high political office. They were elected in more significant numbers and pushed harder for solutions to poverty and access to property. Political factions emerged, and the Senate mishandled the resulting class warfare. The breaking point occurred when Marius (157-86 BCE), commander of the Roman army, removed the property requirement to serve in the military. This change shifted soldiers' loyalty from the Senate, as the people's representative, to the commander, who could pay them for the spoils won in battle.

Now, the army had become a tool of any military leader who sought government control. Fifty years later, Julius Caesar overthrew the republic and took control of the Roman government. After he had been in power for five years, Caesar was assassinated by conservatives who wanted to return to the old system. The killing of Caesar could not stop the momentum for change; twenty years later, the republic was gone.

Conservatism in the Medieval World
Europe regressed to a barbaric state after the last Roman emperor abdicated in 476 CE. One thousand years of Roman civilization were erased: the economy, the laws, and government hierarchies were gone. Then, ever so slowly, Western Europe began to recover, and monarchies emerged as the dominant political system.

The Kingdom of the Franks grew in power in Western Europe and influenced European politics. Alongside them, The Holy Roman Empire evolved, validated by the pope's crowning of Charlemagne, in 814 CE, as its emperor. Later, competing powers emerged in Europe, weakening France, and an alliance between Germany, Italy, Hungary, and

Austria emerged as its principal rival. Feudalism began to appear in France and spread to other parts of Europe.

The early kings of Europe were not powerful enough to fund their armies, so a new type of social hierarchy evolved. Feudalism was a pseudo-governmental system featuring a set of reciprocal obligations between the warrior class and their servants. The lord was a wealthy landowner, and the vassal was an individual seeking protection in return for his loyalty. The vassal was subject to both military and non-military service. An agreement was signed formally between the two parties, including an oath of allegiance to the lord.

Feudalism survived in Germany and France until about 1300 CE. It slowly passed out of existence because kingdoms became more robust, and their armies were made up of mercenaries rather than subjects, negating the effectiveness of the feudal model. Like earlier empires, the feudal system was built on loyalty, authority, and sanctity, all conservative values. Life for the commoner remained a survival-of-the-fittest struggle.

Prelude to the Enlightenment Period
Monarchies were successful in pre-modern society because wealth created power, and power was concentrated at the top of society. Kings and queens were able to maintain power by using hereditary legitimacy. Still, monarchies would not be able to withstand the change coming, a change that would replace authoritarian governments as the most popular model of government.

Three centuries before the Enlightenment, a period of trouble began in Europe. During 1315-1322 CE, a famine killed 10-15% of the people in European towns. Crops failed, farm animals died, people starved, and crime was rampant. The Catholic Church was blamed because the people believed the clergy's prayers were ineffective. Then, in 1347, a pandemic called the Black Death, caused by Bubonic Plague, appeared. Four years later, 40% of the European population was dead. Economies were disrupted because workers were scarce and prices were high.

Amid all this pain, and maybe because of it, a spark was created with a new focus on the inherent value of human life. Humanism evolved as a scholarly approach centered on the analysis of ancient Latin and Greek texts as a way to revive scholarship. Scholars sought to reawaken the ancients' ideas and include them in a new conception of human life. Humanists eventually produced two essential inputs to Enlightenment thinking: A renewed emphasis on scholarship and criticism of abuses by the Catholic Church.

Petrarch (1304-74), considered the first humanist, reacted against what he saw as human ignorance in the centuries preceding his birth, the time known as the Dark Ages. Petrarch sought to revive the ancient works of Cicero and return Europe to the intellectual rigor of antiquity. Erasmus (1466-1536) followed Petrarch a century later. He was a Catholic priest, theologian, and scholar who traveled widely across Europe. Erasmus studied the Bible and produced new interpretations of the sacred text and translations into modern Latin and Greek based on his knowledge of Greek

27

and Latin. These translations gave private individuals access to the Bible, removing their dependency on official church interpretation. Although he retained his loyalty as a Catholic, Erasmus was highly critical of the Catholic super-structure and suggested it carve out a way to try and reform itself.

The Renaissance, which began in the 15th Century, overlapped with the Humanist Period and was a companion to it. Mainly a cultural movement, the Renaissance featured the advancement of art, architecture, and music. Both the Renaissance and the Humanist Period created a foundation for the Enlightenment Period, emphasizing scholarship and art produced by individuals rather than institutions. For the first time since the Greeks, 2,000 years earlier, liberal thinking was active in Western Europe. Scholars and governments would soon focus on the individual as the center of society and the rights that political systems must grant to their people.

CHAPTER FOUR

LIBERAL THINKING EMERGES DURING THE ENLIGHTENMENT

Enlightenment is man's emergence from his self-incurred immaturity. **Immanuel Kant**

In the primitive world, liberal personality types were partnered with their conservative counterparts to seek a consensus on important decisions. Both groups were part of humans' evolutionary adaptation to being social as each played their role: The liberals advocated change and the pursuit of new experiences, while the conservatives argued for the status quo and stability. When agriculture began, human society became a hierarchy, replacing egalitarian social groups. Conservatives were able to take control based on their loyalty and authority-based morality. Liberals found themselves on the sidelines for 5,000 years. A class society with power at the top was the natural human structure for managing a complex society.

As the Enlightenment unfolded, there was an awakening of liberal ideas, which began to compete with the views of conservatives. The result was a change in government structure, replacing authoritarian power with citizens' rights.

Now liberals could seek equal standing in government with conservatives.

In the history of the Western World, the Enlightenment was humankind's most profound and far-reaching intellectual and social advancement.[4] Centered in Europe, the Enlightenment fostered ideas that defined the modern world and provided the founding principles for the American political system. The Enlightenment period saw three major political currents established that have continued to the present: conservatism as a political philosophy, liberalism as a political philosophy, and socialism as an economic and political ideology.

The Enlightenment period was a social and intellectual movement in Europe and North America from 1650 to 1800. People had been told what to think by their church and king, who claimed exclusive access to the will of God and an absolute understanding of how they should live their lives. Knowledge was hoarded by the elites, leaving ordinary people with no way to determine the truth for themselves. Enlightenment thinking replaced this concept with the right of individuals to think for themselves. The resulting freedom facilitated the emergence of science, capitalism, and democracy as foundations for advancing the human species.

From the standpoint of science, the Enlightenment has two parts: The Early Enlightenment (1650-1750) and the Late

---

[4] James MacGregor Burns. *Fire and Light. How the Enlightenment Transformed the World.* St. Martin's Press, New York, 2013

Enlightenment (1750-1800). The advent of science characterized the Early Enlightenment as a discipline and the belief that intuition alone could determine truth. The Late Enlightenment saw intuition discarded as unreliable and false after the philosopher David Hume (1711-1776) demonstrated that humans commonly misinterpret their experiences. Hume destroyed the nationalist ideology of science and forced science to redefine itself. That redefinition, the modern scientific method, has survived to the present day.

The Enlightenment was not a homogeneous movement with a single goal. It was a set of overlapping intellectual activities that influenced the entire range of human experience. It permeated every aspect of human life: religion, politics, economics, science, and, most importantly, the human view of themselves. A universally optimistic endeavor based on the idea of progress, the Enlightenment was a time for intellectual contemplation. Was this new world of free thought a good or bad thing? Would it create risks for humankind if his inventions become impossible to control? Ultimately, Enlightenment society weighed satisfying its curiosity against the dangers that might result and decided the risk was worth taking.

Monarchs were pressured to accept religious tolerance and separate their temporal authority from the spiritual and moral authority of the church. Moreover, the Enlightenment defined new roles for monarchs who sought education to demonstrate that their kingdoms were enlightened.

Rational Thinking

In the early period of the Enlightenment, rationalist thinkers began to dominate philosophy and other academic disciplines, including art, history, and science. Descartes (1596-1650), Spinoza (1632-1677), and Leibniz (1646-1716) were the leading proponents of rationalism, the philosophical view that sees human reasoning as the chief source and test of knowledge. More formally, rationalism was a theoretical foundation stating that the validation of truth was not sensory but was obtained by an internal thought process.

Rationalists argued that certain truths existed without question, and the human intellect could directly understand them. They asserted that specific rational principles existed in logic, mathematics, ethics, and metaphysics; those principles were fundamentally true; thus, denying them would be nonsensical. The rationalists' confidence in reason was so high that they regarded empirical proofs and physical evidence as unnecessary. In other words, one could gain knowledge independently from sensory experience.

As mentioned earlier, David Hume (1711-1776) caused a philosophical revolt during the later period of the Enlightenment. His theory, labeled empiricism, negated the arguments of rational philosophers. Hume asserted that knowledge comes from our perception of the world. Because that perception can be faulty, absolute truth is unknowable. There is no permanence to objects outside of our sense of them.

Immanuel Kant (1724-1804), a rationalist, looked for a way to fit Hume's theories into his own. He put aside rationalism's proof of reality to explore how human beings acquire knowledge. Kant concluded that humans could not know the real world because their senses were separate from the external world. He separated humans' sensory ability from non-sensory knowledge, which cannot be perceived. The concept of God is an example of non-sensory knowledge, so it cannot be proved or disproved.

Rationalists tried to apply new theories of knowledge, but those theories failed when tested by science. Scientists abandoned rationalism in favor of the scientific method, won the battle for truth, and philosophers were left to fight over abstract ideas and forget about the real world.

Individualism

Enlightenment philosophers and scientists believed individualism was awakening the human spirit and a chance for all people to become self-reliant. A person's interests would precede the interests of the state and any group within it. The individual would now be the vehicle to lead the human struggle for liberation, and society must be structured to support that goal.

Science

Before the Enlightenment, science was known as natural philosophy, which included the theoretical study of nature and the physical universe. Its companion discipline was natural history, which involved qualitative and descriptive studies of objects in the world. During the Enlightenment, science separated itself from philosophy and emerged as a separate academic discipline. Its purpose was to gain knowledge from the real world rather than speculate about what it must be like.

From the beginning, Science was a part of the Enlightenment through the work of Francis Bacon (1561-1626 CE), who introduced the scientific method to the world. He believed scientific knowledge should be based on inductive reasoning and careful observation of natural events. Most importantly, Bacon maintained that understanding could be achieved through a skeptical and systematic approach that prevented scientists from misleading themselves. Bacon's method and practical ideas gradually fell out of favor, but he is still considered the father of the scientific method.

Political Theory and Liberalism
With the Enlightenment's emphasis on the individual and its realignment of authoritarian governments and the traditional church, new ideas about political systems emerged. How should humans govern themselves in the new world? Ancient Greek democracy and the Roman Republic stood as examples from the past that featured citizens' rights. Enlightenment thinkers came to believe those models could help design modern political systems.

A new ideology, Classic Liberalism, arose as a political form. Core beliefs of this new system established the idea of a society made up of individuals, departing from the older views of society as a family. Classic Liberals believed that individuals should take the lead in determining how they could succeed in life and have a voice in how their government should be run.

The English philosopher Thomas Hobbes (1588-1679) asserted that the purpose of government was to minimize conflicts between individuals. For example, in a society, courts were granted power from the authorities to resolve issues without violence. In his book *Leviathan*, Hobbes proposed a political system based on absolute government power. Laws were not enough to keep human beings from dangerous behaviors, so authoritarian control was required to act as a deterrent.

John Locke (1632-1704), an English philosopher like Hobbes, exerted significant influence during the Enlightenment. Known as the "Father of Liberalism," Locke believed that the people's consent should rule the government. He disagreed with the pessimism of Hobbes, thinking that human nature was characterized by freedom and tolerance, not evil. Locke's book, *A Second Treatise on Government*, described his views on government structure. Locke believed four principles should bind the government.

First, the government ought to rule by established laws. Second, the legislature could not rule arbitrarily and should abide by the laws it passed to protect the people. Thirdly, the government could not take an individual's property or tax their property unfairly. Fourth, the legislature could not transfer its power to another entity. Locke believed in the separation of powers defined so each branch of government could provide a check on the others. These views had a significant influence on America's founding fathers, who incorporated them into the design of the American government.

Classical Liberals argued for a minimal state, limiting government to protecting individual rights, maintaining national defense, and passing laws protecting citizens from each other.

In the 17th Century, liberal ideas began influencing governments in The Netherlands, Switzerland, England, and Poland. Other states retained the longstanding monarchical forms of government because power was held by those who continued to favor absolute monarchy and established religions. In the 18th Century, America became the first government, in the West, with neither a monarch nor a hereditary aristocracy. The American Declaration of Independence included the famous words:

> All men are created equal; that they are
> endowed by their Creator with certain
> unalienable rights; that among these are life,
> liberty, and the pursuit of happiness; that to
> ensure these rights, governments are
> instituted among men, deriving their just
> powers from the consent of the governed.

The American version of liberalism eventually spread around the globe as a replacement for governments built on aristocratic power.

Capitalism

Drawing on the ideas of Adam Smith (1723-1790), Classic Liberals believed that all individuals should be free to manage their economic self-interests and use that freedom to create new businesses. They thought an entrepreneur should be free to pursue any opportunity to establish a company they felt could bring profitability. It was expected that business owners reap the benefits of success or suffer a penalty if their business failed. Capital was the key to business operations. It took capital to start a trade; if it operated efficiently and effectively, that business would generate profits for its owners.

Classic Liberals argued that individuals should be free to obtain work from the highest-paying employer. The employer's profit motive ensured that popular products were produced at affordable prices. Making money requires businesses to compete for customers and sell products and services. In a free market, labor and capital receive the greatest possible reward, while consumer demand would be an impetus for well-organized and efficient production.

The expansion of capitalism can be traced to the merging of agrarian business and mercantilism during the mid-16th Century. Capital and commercial trade had existed since ancient times, but they did not lead to industrialization or dominate the production systems of society. Modern capitalism required six elements to become established: banks, which could be used to protect profits, extensive production facilities, and workers; technology, which could be used for mass production; the ability for individuals to own the companies they managed; and laws supporting the operation of a business.

The Enlightenment and Conservatives

Most conservatives rejected the Enlightenment because it disrupted the traditions they lived by. The most vocal conservative advocate in Britain was Edmund Burke (1729-1797), a member of the Whig Party. Burke argued for continuing the traditional aristocracy because it was the only way to create the country's future leaders. Burke heavily criticized the French for their revolution, citing it as the best example of why traditions are important. The French people had destroyed their society to gain revenge against the monarchy, the church, and the aristocracy. Then, when all their traditions had been swept away, there was no foundation to build a new government. As a result, political disruption continued for decades, and it took the French 80 years to rebuild a stable political system.

The Enlightenment and Liberals

Although the Enlightenment was best known for its concept of individual freedom and its influence on the emergence of science, capitalism, and democracy, another set of ideas appeared and had an enormous impact on the future of Western society. Socialist concepts emerged, as a rival ideology, to Classic Liberalism (conservativism), joining the fight to control the Western cultural and political landscape. Socialists saw the Enlightenment's focus on the individual as dangerous because it ignored group interests, the traditional model of human culture. That concern generated a new concept of government called socialism, which sought to supersede the emerging capitalist model. To the socialists, the individual was not qualified to dictate the function of government.

Development of Collectivist Thought
The concept of collectivism, developed by socialists, was based on opposition to the Enlightenment. Although labeled a counter-Enlightenment idea, collectivism was not established as a resistance effort, *per se*. It emerged from forces that rejected the new liberal-capitalist model. The strength and power of individualism during the Enlightenment dominated the Western world, and, in the beginning, it had no competitors. The collectivists spent their first 50 years working to build significant opposition. More established by 1800, they began a fight that lasted two centuries and continues today. Since the end of the 20th Century, collectivists have embraced identity politics and postmodernism to attempt to overthrow the Enlightenment's individualism.

Rousseau believed that civilization developed at the expense of morality. To him, the root of moral degradation was reason, as defined by adherents of the Enlightenment. Before they were able to reason, human beings lived simple lives. As time passed, human behaviors led to a surplus of wealth and property rights claims. Property ownership motivated individuals to accumulate wealth at the expense of the less fortunate. Having succeeded in the competition of life, the rich fought to protect their positions and possessions, which expanded the inequality between rich and poor. Rousseau sought to create a society between the modern world and the primitive state. That new state would be governed by religious principles, acting as a stabilizing force. The concept of reason was destructive to society; natural passion ought to replace it. Rousseau's words became manifest during the constitutional phase of the French Revolution when the revolutionaries embraced his ideas.[5]

Both left and right collectivist thinking emerged after Rousseau. These natural opponents were linked by the common desire to oppose the Enlightenment, advocate for strong government, support state religion, show disinterest toward science, and express a firm rejection of violence. For all the differences between left and right collectivists, their common enemy was individualism which, in their view, had cursed the West with capitalism, limited government, separation of church and state, and the belief that economic principles benefit society.

Collectivism in Germany
The Germans were disgusted by the murder of the French king in 1793. Following their defeat by Napoleon, they were convinced the Enlightenment was corrupt and disastrous for humankind. Immanuel Kant (1724-1804) reacted to the times and charted a new philosophical path for the German people.

---

[5] Jean Jacques Rousseau. *Selected Writings*: *The Social Contract, Discourse on the Origin of Inequality, Discourse on the Arts and Sciences, Discourse on Political Economy.* Translated by D.G.H Cole.

Separate from his theory of knowledge, which was anti-reason, Kant lectured on and wrote about many subjects, including physics, anthropology, meteorology, psychology, and history. His advocacy of the Enlightenment appeared in his paper *What is Enlightenment?*[6] Kant called out humankind's laziness and willingness to let others block their reasoning ability. The key to human Enlightenment was freedom, so if society could be constructed to allow individuals to use reason in all matters, humankind could move toward enlightenment. This objective could not be accomplished quickly because changing human behavior takes time.

In contrast to the foundational positions of the Enlightenment, Kant was also an advocate of collectivism and war. In his paper *An Idea for a Universal History with a Cosmopolitan Aim*, Kant defined humankind as a collective. He asserted that, in nature, the individual meant nothing. Nature propelled itself forward mechanically, reacting to the environment and creating new creatures. A single individual within any one species was inconsequential.

In *Idea for Universal History*, Kant stated that war was a valuable tool to carry humans into the future. One outcome of living in society was humans' antagonism toward others, which often led to war. Besides cleansing human society, war was nature's way of bringing forth the higher development of human capacities. In other words, Kant asserted that once the natural antagonism of humans versus

---

[6] Immanuel Kant. *What is Enlightenment?* Konigsberg, Prussia, September 30, 1784.

humans exhausted itself through war, humankind could achieve permanent peace. In Kant's view, war was appropriate and valuable to resolve human conflicts, so the German people must defeat lesser nations who stood in the way.

Hegel

George Friedrich Hegel (1770-1831), a German philosopher, believed that if Rousseau was correct, the Enlightenment notion of freedom was a fraud. Hegel believed all human possessions came through the state. Human history determined what was absolute, whether God, universal reason, or the divine idea. The carrying out of God's plan was human history. The state was the instrument of God's plan, so the duty to the state was more important than the individual.

Hegel, Kant, and other German philosophers were liberals but not Enlightenment liberals. In other words, they were liberal thinkers opposed to the Enlightenment. Enlightenment liberalism became linked to capitalism and became conservative politics. The European political left became socialists and developed their ideology.

Collectivist Models

Henri de Saint-Simon (1760–1825), the founder of French socialism, argued that a society of humans must benefit from the scientific organization of industry. He proposed that the state carry out production and distribution, allowing everyone an equal opportunity to develop their talents, leading to social harmony. If this could be accomplished, the traditional state could be eliminated, replaced by the administration of society.

Charles Fourier

François Marie Charles Fourier (1772–1837) was a French utopian socialist and philosopher who inspired the founding of a utopian communist community, La Reunion, near present-day Dallas, Texas, and several other communities within the United States. Fourier's ideas were attempted in the middle of the 19th Century when hundreds of communes were founded on Fourierist principles in France, North America, Mexico, South America, and Europe. These communities were tribes of shared interest, trying to build a thriving collective community. All failed for various reasons, disagreements about administration and climatic conditions being the most common. In reality, shared interest was only an ideal. Practical living could not overcome people's psychological, temperamental, and intellectual differences, ultimately driving them apart. A society that uses modern egalitarian rules could never emulate the conditions that had worked so well in the primitive world.

The Anarchism of Mikhail Bakunin

Russian-born Mikhail Bakunin (1814-1876) is the father of modern anarchism. He was a libertarian socialist, advocating for workers to manage industrial production directly through their productive associations. These associations would provide welfare programs such as support for all children until they reach maturity and additional resources and facilities to help their transition to adulthood. Many socialists emphasized a gradual transition to the socialist state, but Bakunin believed that approach was ineffective. He supported direct political action as the best way to build a collectivist state.

Bakunin traveled across Europe trying to stir up a socialist revolutionary spirit while advocating the overthrow of the Russian Czar. He was arrested for participating in the Czech Revolution of 1848 and imprisoned in Germany. Later returned to Russia; Bakunin was detained by the Czar and exiled to Siberia. He escaped in 1861 and went to London via San Francisco and Boston. Bakunin attended the first international convention of the Communist Party in 1869 and was active in the party until 1872, when theists expelled him.

The Collectivist Model of Karl Marx
Karl Marx (1818-1883) and Friedrich Engels (1820-1895) were the creators of economic socialism. Their ideas emerged from socialist concepts introduced during the French Revolution, the philosophy of Hegel, the English political economy, and the writings of Adam Smith. Marx and Engels published their famous Communist Manifesto in 1848, the year of revolutions in Western Europe. Marx differed from utopian socialists because he believed that no transition to a socialist state could occur without a class struggle. Marx and Engels believed that achieving a socialist system depended on the workers gaining common ownership of their workplaces. The goal of a communist society was to prohibit bourgeois (middle-class) property. Marx believed that capitalism could only be overthrown

through a revolution by the working class, the only one with the power and motivation to succeed.

For Marxists, socialism was the first phase of communist society; it was a transitional stage characterized by joint, or state, ownership of the means of production under democratic workers' control and management. That stage formed the connector between the capitalist and communist states. Because the socialist phase had characteristics of its capitalist ancestor and the future communist state, it would collectively manage the means of production. It would distribute commodities directly to workers according to their contributions. When the socialist state withered away, the resulting system would be a society where human beings no longer suffered from alienation and all the springs of cooperative wealth flowed abundantly. For Marx, a communist society replaced all social classes and ended class warfare. Once a socialist society was achieved, the capitalist state would end, and humanity would be in control of its destiny for the first time in human history.

Moral Collectivism
While one group of socialists was developing models for collectivist governments, a separate group of moral socialists emerged, advocating a philosophy that equated morality with equality. This philosophy is called utilitarianism, which contains principles attempting to create universal happiness and eliminate harm.

The founder of utilitarianism was the Englishman Jeremy Bentham (1748-1832), a social reformer who actively pursued prison reform, women's rights, sexual rights, and animal rights. Bentham was one of the first to advocate for a welfare state and was also a proponent of abolishing capital punishment and separating church and state.

Bentham believed that the life of humans was determined by the amount of pleasure and pain they experience. He asserted that all human beings want to maximize their pleasure and minimize their pain, so in a society where the economic well-being of people is widely varied, the government must try to maximize happiness and reduce harm among the people.

Bentham chose money to measure happiness to determine the basis for economic redistribution. He noticed that rich people were happier, so it seemed obvious that if the government could increase the wealth of the poor, they'd be happier. Bentham believed that governments must institute systems that distribute wealth throughout society by collecting data on the state of happiness of everyone, compiling that data, and acting on it. Bentham created a table of happiness and harm factors for that purpose.

Bentham's approach received a great deal of criticism based on three points. First, his theory did not consider the human conscience, an essential motivator in decision-making. Conscience could overcome pleasure-seeking in a variety of circumstances. Second, Bentham did not believe in natural rights. He thought human rights were God-given and earthly rights were an illusion. Bentham's critics saw this as an attack on a free society based on natural rights. Third, he was criticized for the lack of true fairness in his model. For example, Bentham's logic could support torturing someone if that act gave greater pleasure to others. The problems with Bentham's utilitarian model would have doomed it without the help of his successor, John Stuart Mill.

John Stuart Mill (1806-1873) was a philosopher and human rights advocate. Mill's father, John (1773-1836), was a well-known Scottish philosopher and Bentham's associate. The elder Mill indoctrinated his son in utilitarian theory. As an adult, the younger Mill rejected Bentham's approach, replacing it with a more comprehensive and practical idea. He sought to reconcile the utilitarian demands of society with a commitment to individual freedom. His famous quote on this was

> ... the sole end for which mankind are warranted, individually or collectively, in interfering with the liberty of action of any of their number is self-protection.[7]

In other words, the government should only act against liberty to prevent harm. Mill rejected Bentham's use of money as a gauge for happiness. He believed that government actions alone could maximize happiness and minimize harm.

---

[7] John Stuart Mill. (1859). *On Liberty*. Batoche Books, Kitchener, Ontario, 2001, Page 13.

Mill suggested a two-step process for happiness/harm decision-making. When a particular action was being considered, it was evaluated to see whether it caused harm. If not, the government was barred from interfering. If the action did cause harm, the government had jurisdiction over whether that action could proceed based on the injury it caused. Mill believed government actions must be applied on a large scale, not individually.

How can the government know where to apply action? There are many cases where the answer is obvious: extortion, blackmail, and assault and battery were typical examples. Others were not so clear. For instance, abortion, prostitution, and denying medical treatment to children for religious reasons depend on one's moral point of view, obscuring the degree of right or wrong.

The modern legal view of this problem divides harm into two forms: harm caused for technical reasons (breaking the law) and harm caused for structural reasons. Fixing structural harm is tricky because it requires agreement on one of two points of view: intentionalist or consequentialist. The intentionalist view says that the individual causing harm intended to do so and should be punished for that reason. The consequentialist point of view ignores the intention in favor of the consequence. For example, an individual strikes another with a baseball bat, but the victim is not severely hurt. The intentionalist would say the perpetrator is guilty because he intended to harm. The consequentialist would say the perpetrator did not harm, so he should not be punished. These issues are not black and white. Depending on their perspective, people can disagree over whether there was harm, so how can the government find solutions to these situations?

Mill believed that as knowledge and education advanced, superstition and irrationality would be replaced by a scientific attitude. That idealistic position has yet to prove to be correct.

Political Impact of the Enlightenment
Conservatives were drawn to capitalism as an Enlightenment concept, focusing on the individual as a valuable member of society. Capitalism was seen as the expression of individuality through entrepreneurship. The right saw capitalism as a tool to successfully manage modern society if it did not infringe on liberty.

The left gained much more from the Enlightenment. It introduced valuing equality and supported government efforts to care for the disadvantaged. It gave the left an ideology that could be used to create the welfare state. The split of collectivists into two economic versus authoritarian camps significantly impacted 20th Century politics. One group sought to build an ideology around economic class differences, driven by a revolution by the working class that would usher in a system of equality. The other group sought an authoritarian political system to control human society from the top.

CHAPTER FIVE

THE WELFARE STATE

*A welfare state, properly conceived, can be
an integral part of a conservative society.*
Irving Kristol

As a feature of modern government, the welfare state was
the logical result of collectivist ideas applied to the post-
Enlightenment Western world. Government welfare is a
modern phenomenon, although it existed in some form as far
back as the Golden Age of Greece. In a welfare state model,
the state protects and promotes its citizens' economic and
social well-being based on the principles of equal
opportunity, equitable distribution of wealth, and public
responsibility for citizens unable to obtain minimal
provisions. That model emerged as part of the
Enlightenment morality rethink. Welfare state policies
reflect an increased role of government as a provider of
services for all citizens. The left has advocated for this
concept because it promotes equality in human society.

As a type of mixed economy, the welfare state funds
governmental institutions for healthcare and education along

with direct benefits given to individual citizens. Early features of this model, such as public pensions and social insurance, were developed in the 1880s in Germany. The Great Depression was a critical event that expanded welfare programs in the United States.

The New Deal programs of Franklin Roosevelt (1882-1945) emerged as a form of state intervention to address unemployment, reverse lost labor output, and affect the recovery of the financial system. The welfare state ideology was carried forward through the 1960s as the Great Society model of Lyndon Johnson (1908-1973). The New Deal's Social Security program and the Medicare program passed in the 1960s, have formed the centerpiece of public services in the United States. Welfare programs, introduced during the Depression, fell out of favor in the late 1970s because of their ineffectiveness. The failure of welfare stigmatized the New Deal liberal ideology as outdated and ineffective.

History of the Welfare State
Emperor Ashoka of India introduced his concept of a welfare state in the 3rd Century BCE. He intended his dharma (religion or path) to be a focus of state policy. Ashoka declared that all men were his children and that his life would be dedicated to discharging his debt to all living creatures. Ashoka renounced war and conquest by violence and forbade the killing of animals. He sent missions across the land to propagate his Dharma. Ashoka's programs included welfare centers for treating people and animals and sites for rest. He prohibited activities that caused waste, laziness, and superstition. To implement these policies, Ashoka recruited

teams of inspectors called Dharmamahamattas to ensure that people of various sects were treated fairly.

Rome

The Roman Republican government sporadically intervened in welfare programs to distribute free or subsidized grain to its population through the program known as Cura Annonae. As the Roman population grew, reaching one million in the 2nd Century CE, poverty and starvation became significant problems.

Regular grain distribution began in 123 BCE via a grain law proposed by Gaius Gracchus and approved by the Roman Plebeian Council (popular assembly). The number of those receiving free or subsidized grain expanded to an estimated 320,000 people at one point. In the 3rd Century CE, bread began to be distributed, replacing grain. Emperor Septimius Severus (193-211 CE) began providing olive oil to residents of Rome, and later Emperor Aurelian (270-275) ordered the distribution of wine and pork. Food distribution continued until the end of the Western Roman Empire in 476 CE. During this period, welfare distribution accounted for as much as fifteen to thirty percent of the total grain imported and consumed in Rome.

Mohammed introduced the concept of states taxing for a welfare budget in the early 7th Century CE. Zakat was a mandatory tax of 2.5% of income paid by all individuals earning a basic threshold. The funds collected were designated for distribution to those in need. Umar (584-644 CE), leader of the Rashidun Caliphate, established a welfare state through the treasury, which was used to stockpile food in every region of the Islamic Empire for disasters and emergencies.

Socialism and the Welfare State in Germany

Germany had the most robust socialist movement in Europe during the early modern period. After 1864 the country became united, and trade unions pressured the German state to create social programs. Carried along by the growing nationalist tide, the socialists organized a political party, positioned themselves to gain power, and worked to transform Germany into a socialist political system.

Opposition parties included the Liberal Party, which sought to form a parliamentary government, the Conservative Party, and the Catholic Party. Although the socialists grew faster than the other parties between 1870 and 1912, their early designs on power were foiled by Otto Von Bismarck (1815-1898). Arguably the most remarkable statesman of all time, Bismarck dominated the affairs of Germany and Western Europe for 30 years between 1860 and 1890. As Minister President of Prussia, Bismarck united the German nation in 1871 and, for the next 20 years, engaged in diplomatic efforts to keep a balance of power between Germany and the rest of Europe.[8]

Bismarck realized that if he embraced specific parts of the Socialist Party agenda, he could disrupt its momentum. To implement his plan, Bismarck broke his alliance with the

---

[8] Edgar Feuchtwanger. Bismarck. London, Routledge Press, 1990.

Liberal Party and aligned himself with the Central Catholic Party. That move allowed him to implement the germ of a welfare state, offsetting the most critical plank in the Socialist Party platform. Bismarck built the German welfare state from the right by diluting the left's power. He also worked with the conservative landowner class to ensure the social changes did not interfere with his traditional conservative power base.

Germany's welfare state efforts were made possible because of the atmosphere in Europe at the end of the Thirty Years' War in 1648. To protect itself from enemies, Prussia began building its army rather than employing mercenaries as the other German states had done. Since the Prussian army's bureaucracy was separate from the government, it grew organically. Then, when the Prussian government decided to implement welfare state programs, the army bureaucracy was available as a platform. Starting with a functioning bureaucracy helped make the new welfare programs permanent and stable.

France
After 1830, liberalism and economic modernization became essential objectives of the French government. Liberalism in the United States and Britain placed its focus on the individual. At the same time, the French followed a unifying conception of society based on the themes of the French Revolution: *Liberté, égalité, fraternité* (liberty, equality, fraternity). Social assistance programs developed in France during the second half of the 19th Century were often initiated by corporations interested to see the welfare state

expand. During the Third Republic (1870-1940), the French government's focus on *Solidarité* (solidarity) was the guiding concept of government social programs. The French welfare state expanded, using the example set by Bismarck. In 1930, France introduced modern social insurance, offering employees protection against accidents, sickness, disability, old age, and death.

Nordic Countries
The Nordic welfare model refers to the welfare state policies of the Nordic countries (Norway, Sweden, and Denmark). Its emphasis on maximizing employment characterizes this model, providing equality-based benefit levels and providing a high percentage of income redistribution. Those benefits can be delivered by charging a high tax rate.

The Nordic countries don't all share the same approach, but they all seek a broad commitment to social cohesion and a universal welfare provision to safeguard individualism. In their view, individualism is best protected when the government maximizes public participation in social decision-making. Nordic systems are characterized by flexibility and openness to innovation and are mainly funded through taxation. Their citizens must accept high tax rates, much higher than Americans.

United Kingdom
Historian Derek Fraser wrote about the British welfare state,

> It germinated in the social thought of late Victorian Liberalism, reached its infancy in the

collectivism of the pre-and post-Great War statism, matured in the universalism of the 1940s, and flowered in full bloom in the consensus and affluence of the 1950s and 1960s. By the 1970s, it was in decline, like the faded rose of autumn.[9]

The modern welfare state in the United Kingdom began with the Liberal welfare reforms of 1906–1914 under Prime Minister H. H. Asquith (1852-1928). These included the passing of the Old-Age Pensions Act of 1908, the introduction of free school meals in 1909, and the Labor Exchanges Act of 1909. The Development and Road Improvement Funds Act of 1909 increased the government's commitment to welfare issues, and the National Insurance Act of 1911 set up a national insurance contribution to cover unemployment and healthcare needs.

In 1909, the United Kingdom introduced a minimum wage for some industries. By the 1920s, reformers offered a new program of family allowance to address continuing poverty. The trade unions and the Labor Party accepted this new concept. In 1945, when family allowances were introduced, minimum wages were discarded. Attempts were made to reintroduce a minimum wage during the Thatcher period, but she rejected them. Later in 1998, a national minimum wage was introduced, with lower rates for younger workers. This wage mainly benefitted workers in high-turnover service

---

[9] Derek Fraser. The evolution of the British welfare state: A history of social policy since the Industrial Revolution. London, Palgrave McMillan, 1973.

industries such as fast-food restaurants and ethnic minorities.

Analysis

Historian of the 20th Century fascist movement, Robert Paxton (1932-), remarked that religious conservatives created the provisions of the British welfare state in the 19th Century to counteract appeals from trade unions and socialism. He writes:

> All the modern 20th Century European dictatorships of the right, both fascist and authoritarian, were welfare states. They all provided medical care, pensions, affordable housing, and mass transport, as a matter of course, to maintain productivity, national unity, and social peace.[10]

Hitler's National Socialist German Workers' Party expanded the welfare state to the point where over 17 million German citizens were receiving assistance under the auspices of the National Socialist People's Welfare by 1939. When social democratic parties abandoned Marxism after World War II, they increasingly accepted the welfare state as a political goal.

---

[10] Robert O. Paxton. "Vichy Lives! – In a way". The New York Review of Books. Archived from the original on 14 April 2013. Retrieved 16 May 2020.

United States

The United States developed a limited welfare state in the 1930s,[11] following the efforts of Lester Frank Ward (1841–1913), the prominent American Sociologist during the Progressive Era. Ward saw social phenomena as amenable to human control. Only through the artificial control of natural phenomena could science minister to human needs. If social laws are analogous to physical laws, there should be no reason why social science can't produce practical applications like physical science. Ward wrote:

> The charge of paternalism is chiefly made by the class that enjoys the largest share of government protection. Those who denounce it are those who most frequently and successfully invoke it. Nothing is more obvious today than the single inability of capital and private enterprise to take care of themselves unaided by the state; and while they are incessantly denouncing paternalism, by which they mean the claim of the defenseless laborer and artisan to a share in this lavish state protection, they are all the while besieging legislatures for relief from their incompetency, and pleading the baby act through a trained body of lawyers and lobbyists. The dispensing of national pap to

---

[11] Walter I. Trattner. From Poor Law to Welfare State, 6th Edition: A History of Social Welfare in America. Free Press, 2007, p. 15.

this class should rather be called maternalism, to which a square, open, and dignified paternalism would be infinitely preferable. [12]

Ward's theories centered around his belief that a universal and comprehensive education system was necessary if a democratic government was to function successfully. His writings profoundly influenced younger generations of progressive thinkers such as Theodore Roosevelt, Thomas Dewey, and Frances Perkins (1880–1965.[13]

The United States was far behind the European countries' welfare state initiatives at the end of the 1920s. The Great Depression shocked American society and forced the government to address the need for welfare state initiatives. Social Security was the most important New Deal initiative, passed in 1935. Social Security was meant to be a pension program that would provide income during the retirement years of working men and women. Its passage was difficult, however, and the program was heavily criticized. Certain groups, including farmers, housekeepers, and non-profit groups, were excluded because they had difficulty finding

---

[12] Lester Frank Ward. Forum XX, Forum 1895. Quoted in Harry Steele Commager's *The American Mind: An Interpretation of American Thought and Character Since the 1880s.* New Haven: Yale University Press, 1950, p. 210.

[13] Henry Steele Commager, Editor. Lester Ward and the Welfare State. New York, Bobbs-Merrill, 1967.

coverage for them. State employees were excluded and later created their own pensions systems.

Several welfare state programs have been implemented since the New Deal Era, including Medicare and Medicaid, Welfare, food stamps, and child nutrition programs. The last holdout was national health insurance, which has eluded passage since the Truman administration tried to pass it in 1948. Finally, in 2010, the Affordable Care Act was passed. The ACA is imperfect and has some uniquely American features, a complex mix of federal, state, philanthropic, employer, and individual funding. Still, it added coverage for some groups who lacked coverage previously. A single-payer plan could not withstand the forces allied against it, including healthcare corporations, insurance companies, and lobbyists. Still, the US spent 16.7% of its GDP on health care in 2019 compared to 11.06% in France and 11.70% in Germany.

Why has the United States trailed the European nations in welfare state development? Labor unions in the United States have always been weaker than their European counterparts. The labor movement in Germany forced Bismarck's government to yield to demands to increase its power. In addition, the Southern United States never had a tradition of unionization because it was not industrialized until recently. Northern unions did not have enough leverage to force the government to respond to their demands. As neoliberalism took hold in the United States, the expansion of capitalism became the country's highest priority, and the welfare system was ignored.

Has the United States caught up to the other Western nations deploying the welfare state? Yes and no. While some aspects mimic programs in other countries, others, notably healthcare, still need to improve. The American healthcare system, which includes the most sophisticated technologies and specialties, is the most expensive. It remains to be seen whether that system can ever be transformed into one like Canada or Germany. To do so would require Americans to give up the rapid service model they currently enjoy.

Percent GDP spent on selected social programs

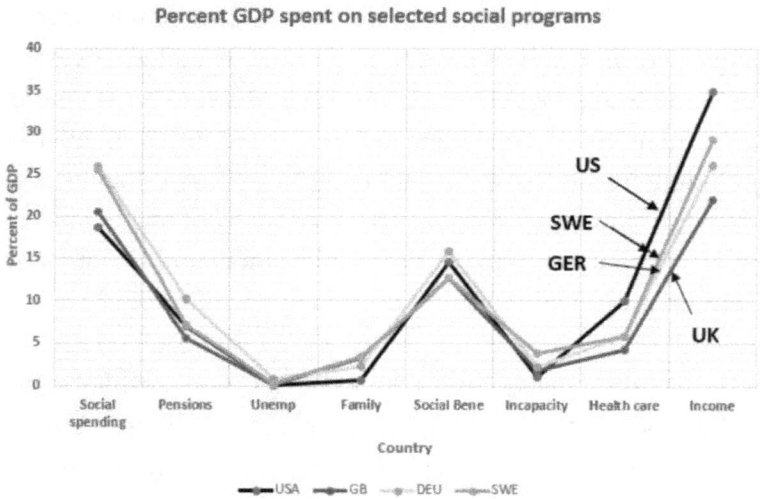

Figure 1. Percent GDP spent on social programs (left axis). Per capita income in thousands (right axis).

A comparison between the United States and representative Western European democracies regarding the percent of GDP spent on specific services shows no significant variation. The right-hand data point compares each country's income in dollars using the numbers from the left axis. For example, the average income in the United States is $ 35,000.

Welfare state implementation is a permanent political activity that has changed the structure of the American Republic. Modeled initially on Enlightenment individualism, the American political system has become more of a collectivist model. The original principles of the Constitution were replaced: positive rights and group focus were substituted for negative rights and individualism. This action is a result of pressure from the political left.

The American welfare state is a compromise between capitalists and socialists over designing a modern political system. Capitalists wanted a system with few welfare elements; they believed modern society should operate as a survival of the fittest. Socialists wanted an egalitarian society where the government provided services that leveled the economic opportunities for all.

CHAPTER SIX

SOCIALIST IDEOLOGY MATURES

The socialist system will eventually replace the capitalist system; this is an objective law independent of man's will. However much the reactionaries try to hold back the wheel of history. Eventually, the revolution will take place and will inevitably triumph.
Mao Tse-Tun

European Socialism After 1850

The word socialism was never the exclusive property of the left because right-wing collectivists also used it. Both were anti-individualists; both advocated government management of the most critical aspects of society; both divided human society into groups deemed fundamental to individuals' identities; both pitted those groups against each other to create conflict; both favored war and violent revolution to bring about the ideal society. This period saw intense nationalistic fervor spread across Europe. Socialists vigorously opposed the Enlightenment and developed tools to attack Enlightenment individualism. They hoped socialist nations could be established by the turn of the 20th Century.

The development of left-wing socialism in Germany was discussed in the previous chapter as it related to the welfare state. Despite the setbacks from Bismarck, the socialist movement continued to expand and gain strength. After 1885, however, it competed with right-wing socialism, which viewed the world through a collectivist lens. German right-wing socialists carried forward the ideas of Herder and Fichte, who preached nationalism, unification, and educational programs that would unite the German nation against all who would harm her. After Bismarck left the scene, the right-wing socialists became more nationalistic. Its shared nationalist ideas eventually led to it merging with the German Liberal Party. A few years later, the Catholic Party joined that coalition.

From the German point of view, World War I was a test of socialist ideology against Enlightenment Liberalism, which Germany never accepted. They were confident that liberalism would not be able to stand up to an authoritarian political system. The defeat of Germany by the Allies forced the German socialists to consider capitalist democracies as legitimate adversaries.

When World War I ended, right-wing Germans adopted a pre-fascist stance, positioning themselves against the working class, represented by left-wing socialists, whom they now rejected. Fascism refers to a political system focused primarily on nationalism and racism. The repositioning replaced the old-style nationalists with a more modern version. The new party, the German National People's Party (DNVP), advanced the right-wing socialist banner and replaced the obsolete Fatherland party. The DNVP was eventually replaced by the Nazi Party, which canceled all other parties after Hitler came to power. When the German people voted the right-wing socialists (Nazis) into power, they chose them over the left-wing socialists (communists).

A New Path for Left-Wing Socialists

While right-wing collectivism expanded in Germany in the 1920s, left-wing socialists tried to understand why they could not progress. Why had the predictions of revolution not come to pass? The exploitation and alienation of the people were apparent, and these victims of capitalism suffered. Still, there was no revolution.

Lenin adapted Marxian theory to account for the differences between Russia and the classic Marxian model in Russia. As a feudal society, Russia had never reached the capitalist state that Marx had predicted in his model of communist evolution. Lenin knew he didn't have time to develop a capitalist model, so he had to make his revolution work without one. That could only be accomplished by creating a new class of socialist elites who could impose the communist doctrine on the Russian people through any means necessary. As the world understood later, Russia evolved into a Marxist authoritarian dictatorship.

The Frankfurt School

In Germany, the German Social Democrats (SPD) proved ineffective, even though they were the largest socialist party in the world. Party intellectuals decided that socialism needed a new direction and leadership who would critique and update the Marxist ideology. That path required new ideas that would replace the ones that failed. The solution came from the Frankfurt School, the educational institution of social theory and philosophy associated with the Institute for Social Research at the Goethe University in Frankfurt, Germany.

The school was made up of neo-Marxist dissidents who were intellectually uncomfortable with the political ideologies at the time. Given its dehumanizing and exploitative character, they questioned why traditional Marxian theory could not explain the capitalist expansion in the 20th Century. Critical of capitalism and Soviet socialism, the Frankfurt School sought an alternative path to socio-political development.

Responding to the alienation and irrationality in an advanced capitalist society, the Frankfurt School developed Critical Theory as a comprehensive, ideology-critical, historically self-reflective philosophical tool with a dual purpose. First, it sought to explain domination in human society, specifically why class separation and alienation exist. Second, it sought to explore the possibility of creating a more rational, humane, and free society. Frankfurt School theorists developed numerous hypotheses and principles of the economic, political, cultural, and psychological structures to explain the operation of advanced industrial civilizations, intending to use them to design an alternative system.

Critical Theory was introduced by Max Horkheimer (1895-1973), one of the Frankfurt School's leaders, in his 1937 book *Traditional and Critical Theory*. The book described the theory and how it could be used. Its author had two objectives: unmask the lies generated by the bourgeois society, which justified the domination of people by capitalism, and explain how changes in human society in the 20th Century had impacted Marx's ideology.

Horkheimer argued that the scientific methodology applied to the physical sciences could not be used in the social sciences because academic researchers were social. In other words, they lost objectivity because their ideas influenced their work. In addition, social science researchers lived in the historical context of their discipline, which shaped their thinking. Horkheimer's solution to this dilemma was the reflective assessment and critique of society and culture using social sciences and humanities knowledge. To overcome the problem of subjectivity in social scientific inquiry, Critical Theory placed itself outside "the box."

Horkheimer asserted that Critical Theory must concentrate its energy on all of society rather than workers only. To gain the proper perspective, it should integrate all the major social sciences, including geography, economics, sociology, history, political science, anthropology, and psychology. For it to provide value, Critical Theory must be able to identify problems in current society and suggest ways they can be fixed. Dedication to that purpose would help humankind escape from the capitalist systems that held it captive.

Frankfurt School theorists affiliated themselves with the critical philosophy of Immanuel Kant, who had used the term *critique* to mean thinking about how knowledge is acquired and how it impacts human moral decision-making. The Frankfurt School theorists would use "critique" to update Marx for the 20th Century.

Critical Theory rejected the materialism of orthodox Marxism. The material tensions and class struggle of which Marx spoke no longer had the same revolutionary potential within contemporary Western societies. That suggested Marx's interpretations and predictions needed to be completed or corrected. Frankfurt School theorists argued that the theory guiding an ideology must be reviewed when its implementation fails. In other words, socialist philosophical thought must be able to criticize itself and repair its errors.

Hope for Victory

The Great Depression in the United States brought hope to socialists worldwide that it would inspire a revolution of the oppressed working class in the United States. That didn't happen. Equally alarming was the rise of National Socialism in Germany and Italy, where movement leaders convinced their public that an authoritarian approach to a government founded and built upon a right-wing socialist ideology was superior to their former governments. The left-wing socialists hoped that right-wing socialists and capitalists would destroy each other during World War II and leave the left-wing socialists to take over. To their surprise, right-wing socialism was damaged, and the liberal West emerged more robust and self-confident from the war than ever. That mixed blessing left the socialists with a single competitor but a formidable one.

Until the mid-1950s, the left was under the illusion that the Soviet Union would prove itself to be a leading economic model and the envy of the world, but, year after year, the Soviet five-year plans failed to produce the results they sought. Once the left understood that the Soviet Union could not win economically, it decided to focus on equality as the desired outcome of socialism. The hope that the Soviet Union might succeed as a morally legitimate ideology died when Soviet Premier Nikita Khrushchev gave a secret speech to the Soviet Party Congress on February 25, 1956, outlining the crimes of Stalin. In October of that same year, the Soviets brutally suppressed an uprising in Hungary. The world could now see that the Soviet Union was nothing more than a violent authoritarian dictatorship with a socialist veneer.

Disappointment over the Soviet failure caused many socialists to embrace Mao, the leader of China, hoping his model would succeed where the Soviets had failed. Again, there was only disappointment when the death toll of 36 million people resulting from Mao's forced famine of 1959-1961 became public. Belief in the legitimacy of the Maoist ideology evaporated.

These disappointments of the 1950s forced most left-wing intellectuals to recognize the case for left-wing socialism was in serious trouble economically and morally because capitalist countries were setting a standard. It was hard to argue with prosperity, and it was hard to make criticisms about the immorality of capitalism when compared to the horror of socialism in practice.

A New Socialist Strategy

A new program was introduced at the party conference of the German Social Democrats (SPD) in November 1959. The Godesberg Program was designed to recast the socialist ideology from defenders of people experiencing poverty, as described in Marxist theory, to an ideology representing all people.

The Godesberg Program was notable because it discarded Marxist materialism and class struggle theories. Moreover, the SPD dropped its hostility to capitalism, which had long been the core of its ideology. Socialism now moved beyond its traditional working-class base to embrace all voters. The new strategy was grounded in ethical appeals rather than economic ones. Labor unions withdrew their demands for nationalization and began to cooperate with industry. Union leaders achieved labor representation on corporate boards and garnered increases in wages and benefits. After losing national elections in the 1950s, the SPD changed to an American-style election strategy that stressed personalities over ideology. As it prepared for elections in 1961, the party dropped its opposition to rearmament and accepted NATO. Previously, it had adhered to the Communist Party edict, opposing all institutions representing the West.

Other approaches appeared as the Frankfurt School rewrote the socialist ideology, focusing on poverty and its demotivating effect on the poor. The assertion was that the working classes would become revolutionary once they understood the injustice of wealth distribution in their societies.

A second approach involved breaking down Marxist theory to focus on special interest groups, specifically women and racial minorities. Emphasis was placed on equality above class identity to attack capitalism. No one could argue that women and racial and ethnic minority groups were making enough progress in capitalist nations.

Marcuse and the Captive Class
Herbert Marcuse (1889-1976), a former member of the Frankfurt School, rose to prominence in the 1960s by taking Marxist theory in a new direction. The American New Left embraced his work, and he gained a significant following. Politically, he was a Marxist, dedicated to embedding the Marxist belief system into the capitalist model.

Marcuse and his contemporaries from the Frankfurt School looked for new ways to replace the class struggle ideology of Marx. They expanded their thinking beyond Marx's social model and sought the answer in psychology. Freud was the prominent psychologist of the time, so Horkheimer and Marcuse used Freud's concepts to develop a new approach.

The Frankfurt School theorists used Freud's 1930 book *Civilization and Its Discontents* as a resource for new ideas.

Freud saw human society as the suppressor of humans' natural behavior, which demanded immediate gratification and behavior without discipline. He suggested that the best way to understand these suppressed urges was to draw them out using non-rational mechanisms, including dream analysis and hypnosis. The Frankfurt School theorists believed that modern capitalist society hid the natural state of humans by creating an artificial world of machines and bureaucracies. Those systems removed human beings from nature and forced them into an unnatural existence, destroying human spontaneity and creativity. Most importantly, people were unaware that this was happening to them.

Marcuse asserted that the wealth generated from capitalism was the oppressor of the working class. By making its members wealthy enough to become comfortable, capitalism had made them captive to wealth-seeking psychology. Once part of the system, the working class locked themselves into a dog-eat-dog existence, constantly competing with their neighbors. Trapped in this process, they were distracted by the material trappings of a capitalist society, foolishly believing that possessions had value. If those chains of oppression could be removed from the backs of the workers, they'd be free to pursue a life of socialism. It was the task of socialist intellectuals to explain how the working class was being exploited so they could see the truth and use it as motivation to achieve a socialist reality.

Terrorism

In the late 1960s, five elements combined to ignite a more violent, terroristic, leftist trend: the academic climate against reason; impatience about the revolution; extreme disappointment at the failure of the socialist ideal; hatred of the success of capitalism; and justification of irrational violence based on the writings of the Frankfurt School. In addition to these factors, several important events triggered the upsurge in violence. Among the far left, the death of Che Guevera (1928-1967) in 1967 and the failure of the 1968 student demonstrations, especially the revolts in France, contributed to radicals' anger and disappointment. Several terrorist manifestos published after 1968 mention those events and reflect the broader themes of irrational will, exploitation, descent from beauty to commodity, rage, and simply needing to do something. For example, Pierre Victor (1945-2003), the French Maoist leader, and friend of the postmodernist Michel Foucault, recalled the French Revolution's Reign of Terror, declaring that instituting a brief period of terror was entirely justified if directed against a handful of vile, hateful individuals.

The new terrorists cast their nets broadly. Ulrike Meinhof (1934-1976) clarified the purpose of the Red Army Faction she and Andreas Baader (1943-1977) had founded in Germany. If it were to be successful, the anti-imperialist struggle required annihilation, destruction, and the shattering of the imperialist power system - political, economic, and military.

Nauseated by the proliferation of the conditions they found in the system, the total commercialization, and absolute corruption in all areas of the superstructure and deeply disappointed by the actions of the student movement and extra-parliamentary opposition, militants, such as the Red Army, many thought it essential to engage in an armed struggle. They wanted to protect the ideas attained by the movement of 1967-1968 and not let the struggle fall apart again.

The rise of left terrorism in nations other than those controlled by explicitly Marxist governments was a striking feature of the 1960s and early 1970s. The broader turn of the left to non-rationalism, irrationalism, and physical activism during that era made the terrorist movement the most contentious and bloody in the history of the left socialist movements of those nations.

But the liberal capitalists were not soft and complacent. By the mid-1970s, police and military forces had defeated the terrorists, killing some, imprisoning many, and driving others underground, more or less permanently. The mid-1970s dispersed the prominent terrorist organizations, and terror lost momentum when the Viet Nam War ended.

With the collapse of the New Left, the socialist movement was dispirited and in disarray. No longer were they waiting for socialism to materialize. No one thought it could be achieved by appealing to the electorate. No one was able to mount a coup. And those willing to use violence were dead, in jail, or underground. What was the next step for socialism?

Seeking alternatives, Marxists in the United States began to think about the writings of the Italian philosopher Antonio Gramsci (1891-1937). Gramsci, a dedicated Marxist, was an independent thinker who had expanded on the ideas of Lenin. Gramsci provided a roadmap for the American Left to pursue its objectives through the university system. The key to this roadmap was understanding Lenin's definition of *hegemony*. Hegemony generally refers to the dominance of one country over another, but Lenin used the term to mean the technique used by capitalist systems to keep control of society. The bourgeoise propagated its values as the only legitimate ones, which helped keep them in power.

Gramsci suggested modern Marxists develop their own culture to compete with the capitalists. That culture must offer an equal attraction for those interested in change. Gramsci respected religion as a component of bourgeoise hegemony, so any thriving counterculture needs to incorporate that essential cultural component.

The Soviet/Marxist Playbook in Operation
Apart from their efforts in the university system, American Marxists have directly pursued attacks on the American political system. These attacks are designed to undermine and weaken American society from within.

In 1984, an ex-Soviet KGB agent, Yuri Bezmenov (1939-1993), described a strategy titled *Soviet Subversion of the*

Free World Press. His presentation included the methods used by the KGB to undermine the American political system. The plan consists of four stages: demoralization, destabilization, crisis, and normalization.

Demoralization

The Marxist demoralization strategy unfolds when schools come under the control of disciples of the left who indoctrinate students in a set of values and beliefs foreign to the American tradition. This process began in the 1960s and 1970s when student radicals took control of educational institutions intending to discard traditional Judeo-Christian morality, classical education, and American patriotism. It has accelerated recently with the emphasis on Critical Race Theory, woke issues, and sexuality being defined as essential to American culture.

This cultural Marxist project operates in media and entertainment outlets that are already opposed to the traditions of our country. The entertainment industry has been left-leaning since communists infiltrated it in the 1940s. Today, it remains closely aligned with the current left-wing progressive ideology. In Hollywood today, two types of films are produced: political and non-political. The political ones get the awards nominations, are popular among ideologues, and don't make any money. The popular ones are highly profitable and are never nominated because they are typically apolitical. Movies have always offered the public a brand of escapism, a chance to take a break from the stresses of everyday life, but few want to attend movies full of political messaging. To the left ideologues, movie attendance doesn't matter because they get satisfaction from emphasizing the unfairness and inequality of American society.

A second area of focus is the "environmental crisis." Warnings about the existential threat of global warming inundate the airwaves. These repetitive warnings are demoralizing, no matter where the truth may lie. The environmental crisis is the perfect political issue because it can't be disproven.

Demoralization is designed to attack and remove what is familiar, including the veneration of traditions. Tearing down statues, criticizing history books, discarding the classics, and changing the curricula to include ideological elements are part of the methodology. Eliminating Christmas and other holidays that carry forward our country's traditions are also priorities.

Demoralization is depressing and confusing, making people believe that the way of life they cherish is ending. We repeatedly hear how our ancestors exploited and abused the people of their time. Those most susceptible to this propaganda feel anxious and want to apologize for sins that are not their own.

Destabilization
Bezmenov described destabilization as a rapid decline in the structure of a society - law and order, the economy, and the political system.

Law enforcement in the United States has been under attack for the past several years. Undoubtedly, there have been abuses by the police, including excessive force, but this problem has been a racial issue and destabilized neighborhoods and cities. In May 2020, this trend came to a head with the George Floyd killing in Minneapolis. Riots destroyed parts of that city, and an effort commenced to defund the police. Law and order were suspended, destabilizing the city to force change. The result of this effort was predictable; crime increased dramatically. In Seattle and Portland, riots continued for months during the summer of 2020. Rioters in Seattle set up a no-police zone where they claimed control, assuming the role of police. This incident was nothing less than a state of anarchy.

In 2021, San Francisco sought to decriminalize certain illegal activities. Shoplifting of less than $800 would not be prosecuted. Gangs began to enter stores, gather merchandise, and walk out without being confronted. Automobile break-ins were rampant within the city. Residents were forced to decide whether to barricade themselves into their homes or hire private security.

The American economy has experienced a period of severe destabilization after the COVID pandemic reached the United States in February 2020. That spring, the economy was shut down, healthcare systems overloaded, and death rates soared. Some segments of the economy rebounded after a few months after the national shutdown, but others remained closed. To make matters worse, the politicization of the pandemic forced Americans to take sides over the best way to control the spread of the disease.

Liberal states were much more aggressive in controlling people's movements and business operations. At first, these controls seemed reasonable, but later they separated from the science. Teachers' unions politicized vaccine availability and refused to work until all teachers were vaccinated. Most schools were shut down during the school year of 2020-21, leaving students to learn remotely. Many Americans have rebelled against the draconian rules of some of the blue states. Red states employed looser controls to avoid damage to their economies. Lawsuits were filed in some states opposing government controls.

Crisis
The COVID pandemic produced a crisis in the United States during the first half of 2020. The economy stopped, the disease caused fear throughout the country, schools were closed, and people were out of work.

Politically, America experienced its third presidential impeachment in American history in February 2020, coincidental with the pandemic, a constitutional crisis that was wholly and completely manufactured without evidence. The first impeachment was followed by a second attempt to impeach Trump *after* he had been defeated in the November 2020 election. By then, the COVID pandemic had been going on for ten months.

The George Floyd riots and the ensuing outbursts of country-wide violence exacerbated the recent campaign to rewrite American history and culture increasingly indiscriminately. The speed of the cultural collapse that followed Floyd's death - when the legal system moved very swiftly against the police officers responsible - makes it undeniable that this was purposeful and only needed a catalyst to support its implementation.

No one could have imagined this convergence of crises happening simultaneously in American society. That was the scenario the left hoped for.

Normalization
The new normal involves reforming the American political system and its social structure. Free market capitalism will be brought under control through taxes and government regulation. Corporations must adhere to government policies on energy conservation and renewable energy. Failure to follow government policies will result in heavy fines and loss of business control. Executive compensation will be capped to maintain a fixed income ratio to the average worker.

A more significant portion of the federal budget will be applied to social programs: free public college, free housing, and credits for buying food. Increased minimum wage and a guaranteed minimum income will be operational. All healthcare will be free, along with family leave and childcare. Expansion of union membership will be mandated to increase the power of unions in the United States. This expansion will be done under the guise of protecting workers' rights.

Equality laws will be strictly enforced, and suits will be brought against anyone who exercises any form of discrimination. School books will be revised, excluding traditional materials and emphasizing equality. White people will be labeled outcasts because of the evil traditions they created and supported: slavery, poverty, and homelessness. The government's objective will be to reduce white people's influence in favor of historically disadvantaged groups.

The radical left actively utilizes that playbook. Socialism is the goal, even though the word must be whispered to hide the truth. The left believes they can succeed, so they are relentless.

The message of Bezmenov has been public for 39 years now. The strategy behind it has been in place since the 1930s. The American people must recognize this effort for what it is and not fall prey to the attacks on our nation. Progressives, as well as traditional liberals, need to understand that their goal of a welfare state needs to be implemented as a part of the capitalism/democracy model. Allowing a radical approach to proliferate opens the door for the socialists.

CHAPTER SEVEN

ACADEMIA MOVES TO THE LEFT

Materialist philosophies that treat human beings as machines or animals possess the high ground in our culture - academia, the most powerful media, and many of our courts. **Marvin Olasky**

The academic ideal implemented almost 400 years ago at American universities was discarded during the 1990s. That decision marked the departure from higher education's historical and traditional role of teaching students to think and prepare for the real world when they graduate. Tradition has been replaced by indoctrination, focused on identifying oppressed groups and incorporating their problems into an expanding left ideology.[14] To the left, the political and ideological game was more important than helping members of the selected groups because their priority gave them political power. Identity groups were merely tools to institutionalize and spread progressive and socialist ideologies.

---

[14] Roger Kimball *Tenured Radicals*. Chicago, Ivan R. Dee, 1990.

Who was to blame for these developments? Indeed, liberal professors teaching in the 1960s were culpable. Those educators (and their bosses in the administration) were spineless in the face of the student protest movement. One could argue whether this resulted from a weakness in liberal ideology or a lack of backbone when faced with a crisis. Critics of liberalism argued for the former as Roger Kimball did:

> Liberalism's tendency to let tolerance and openness trump every other virtue renders it particularly impotent when faced with substantive moral dilemmas: absolutized, tolerance and openness become indistinguishable from moral paralysis. We know for a certainty that the liberal capitulation of university administrators in the Sixties and Seventies helped enormously to establish – and institutionalize – the radical ethos of the counterculture. [15]

Radicalization

In the 1960s, during a period of changing morality and attitudes in America, student radicals were thinking about ways to implement Karl Marx's ideas. Still, they were frustrated that America lacked an oppressed working class. They could see that American workers and farm communities were fundamentally conservative. Without a disenchanted working class to exploit, student radicals

---

[15] Roger Kimball. *The Long March*. San Francisco, Encounter Books, 2000, p 106.

decided *they* were the oppressed class: forced to join the army and be killed in Vietnam, lacking the right to vote, and discouraged from participation in the sexual revolution.

The flashpoint of the counterculture movement was the Berkeley protests in 1964, which began as a fight over a piece of land on the Berkeley campus, students used for political action. The university decided the land was subject to its rules and regulations, so they had the right to prohibit student activities there. The implementation of these rules led to a wave of student anger. In a notable speech on December 2, 1964, student Mario Savio (1942-1996) supported student resistance.[16] He asserted that students must refuse to be treated like gears in a machine subject to the university administration's whims. They needed to put themselves inside those gears and make them stop. Their method of action would not include violence; it would be peaceful, organized sitting in protest. Savio's speech led to increased demonstrations at Berkeley, aimed at creating an anti-establishment narrative that labeled American morality as corrupt.

Similar protests followed at Columbia University, Yale, and Cornell. Time Magazine stated, "The general pattern that emerged was irresponsible, self-aggrandizing license on the part of students; fretful collaboration on the part of faculties;

---

[16] Mario Savio. Bodies Upon the Gears Speech. https://www.youtube.com/watch?v=xz7KLSOJaTE&ab_channel =IndridCold

pusillanimous [cowardly] capitulation on the part of administrators."[17]

During the late 1960s, affirmative action programs were implemented at American universities to increase the number of black students attending majority-white institutions. As these programs got underway, there were complaints that American universities' white or Eurocentric culture handicapped black students. Dissidents demanded that universities create Afro-American and Afro-centric programs. In a foreshadowing of identity politics in the 21st Century, Black students at Cornell accused a visiting Professor of Economics of racism because he made the mistake of judging the development of African nations by Western standards. The administration forced the professor to apologize, but Black students were unsatisfied, so they took control of the Economics Department office and held the chairman and his secretary hostage for 18 hours. An investigating Dean found the professor innocent but accused the university of institutional racism. There was a single case of purported racism growing into an attack on academia.[18]

The counterculture movement ultimately became radicalized into an oppressed versus oppressor ideology. The followers of this emerging ideology were not interested in the individual, only the individual's category, be it race, gender group, or class. By their definition, every American was

---

[17] Harvard and Beyond: *The University under Siege*. Time Magazine April 18, 1969, p.47.

[18] Kimball, Roger. *The Long March*. 113.

either an oppressor or a member of an oppressed group. Group membership was a person's label, replacing all other characteristics. Wealthy and educated Blacks were oppressed, and poor whites were the oppressors. In this scenario, the only way to escape the role of the oppressor was to defend the rights of the oppressed. The oppressors included parents and all the establishment, the military-industrial complex, and religious people who support the dominant, traditional culture. Over time, radicals expanded the list of oppressed groups to include Latin Americans and women.

Before the 1960s, student behavior had followed what many called a *middle path*, a set of unwritten rules for student conduct that placed a brake on unlimited freedom. The middle path included such intangible concepts as fairness, duty, judgment, and taste. Tradition held that adherence to the middle path was a good measure of the strength of any university. The 1960s saw department after department at great American universities respond to student requests for emancipation by casting aside tradition in favor of the New Left ideology. University administrations accepted the radical left agenda as not only appropriate but as the foundation for redesigning their institutions. By the end of the 1960s, the radical left agenda had been institutionalized in American universities, and the middle path was abandoned in favor of political agendas.

Events around the world helped shape the final years of the 1960s. The year 1968 was extraordinarily turbulent because the left's tactics moved from protests, sit-ins, and riots to terrorism. On March 11, President Johnson, facing criticism over his handling of the Vietnam War, announced he would not run for a second term. On April 2, bombs exploded in Parisian department stores, igniting a new level of terrorism. The Red Army Faction, a radical group from Germany, who was reacting against the Vietnam War, had planted those bombs. On April 4, Martin Luther King was assassinated. On May 13, student riots broke out in Paris. On June 5, Robert Kennedy was assassinated. On August 20-21, an invading Russian army put down the Prague Spring liberalization in Czechoslovakia. August 22-30 saw student riots at the Democratic Convention in Chicago.

By the end of 1968, Marxists around the world were disappointed. The Soviet Union had put down the revolt in Czechoslovakia, showing itself as an enemy of freedom. The death toll from Mao's enforced famine became public, and respect for Mao as a model socialist was destroyed. The Soviet Union and China were now seen as corrupt political systems rather than socialist models to be emulated. With no models to emulate, the left moved in a different direction. That direction involved adapting their ideology to change the capitalist system rather than replace it by force.

As mentioned in the previous chapter, radical professors and students began to think about the writings of the Italian philosopher Antonio Gramsci. They heeded Gramsci's words about the need for an ideological alternative to capitalism. Marxists in the United States teamed up with university professors and activist students to help guide the implementation of Gramsci's plan. The plan was built from the ashes of the New Left movement by institutionalizing Gramsci in academia. Using an oppressor-oppressed dichotomy, the anti-establishment focus formed the beginning of their battle against capitalism.

Influence of Postmodernism

American universities began discarding their traditional views, in the early 1970s, under the influence of the Postmodernist movement. A group of French philosophy professors, including Michel Foucault (1926-1984), Jacques Derrida (1930-2004), and Francois Lyotard (1924-1998), came to the United States to preach the ideology of postmodernism. All were formerly associated with the French Communist Party. All believed the world had reached the end of the Modern Age and was transitioning to a new cultural model, replacing Enlightenment thinking. According to the postmodernists, these factors had created a new kind of cultural and social life in the Western world. The speed of communications disrupted humankind's ability to function through thoughtful planning and careful implementation of new ideas, so a new way of thinking was called for.

Postmodernism became a part of popular culture through its focus on distraction, interest in discarding the past, and emphasis on the meaninglessness of life. Postmodernists successfully described the world in a way that other ideologues did not. Socialism and liberalism have always depended on an agreement about the source of problems in a political society to validate solutions against those sources.

91

In the 1970s, that approach didn't seem to be working anymore.

Many, including feminists and gay activists, focused on the work of Michel Foucault because of his unique views on the social construction of sexuality, power, and the connection between power and knowledge. Those groups saw Foucault's work as providing a theoretical ground for moving away from a focus on the economy and the state to the social relations between people and the problems of daily life. Foucault viewed state power as repressive, and his kinship with the marginalized and suppressed rang true with groups leading radical struggles outside the mainstream of culture and power relations. As time moved on, especially in the 1980s, postmodernism became associated with *avant-garde* or trendy currents. It acted out its new role by adopting criticism for its own sake and moved away from its connection to social movements. New links were created with academia, so postmodernism expanded its position in elite universities. There, it became subject to the harsh and competitive research world and the need to publish or perish. Postmodernism accomplished that by standing out, bringing attention to itself, and advocating radical behavior.

The effects of Postmodernism on academic disciplines depended on the field and its foundational principles. Pure sciences rely on truth, so extreme positions questioning its existence did not gain much traction. Art and architecture reflect postmodernist ideas but use their definitions, separate from postmodernist philosophy. There are legitimate reasons for characterizing a period of art as postmodernist, reflecting a period after modernism based on the evolution of art from a previous point in history. The same holds for architecture which created a postmodernist style as a reaction against the staleness of the architecture of the 1970s. Many social sciences and humanities disciplines have absorbed postmodernism into their fields because they needed a theoretical foundation. They were attracted to using postmodernism as a framework for their fields. For example, English programs adopted the postmodernist tool of deconstruction to create a new way of analyzing texts.

Postmodernism became the primary field of knowledge for education at the elite colleges of the United States. It is a vital component of about two dozen different disciplines, subfields, and areas of study, including Cultural Studies, Postcolonial Studies, Rhetoric and Composition, English Literature, French Literature, American Studies, Film Studies, Women's Studies, Ethnic Studies, Queer Theory, Media Studies, Communications, Music Theory, Science and Technology Studies, Theater and Performance Studies, Anthropology, Continental Philosophy, and Theology. Even in the social sciences – sociology, economics, geography, psychology, and political science – among those academics who identify with the emancipatory or 'critical' tradition, postmodernism sits on at least equal ground with Marxism as the preferred ideology.[19]

Those disciplines that embraced Postmodernism after the mid-1970s are in a crisis. Their research output is dubious,

---

[19] John Sanbonmatsu. *The Postmodern Prince*. New York, Monthly Review Press, 2004.

driven by a postmodernist point of view, which lacks foundational concepts. The "intellectual" bias of postmodernism has been publicized to American society through public sector institutions and the media, although it offers nothing positive to the American cultural narrative. In the 1970s, postmodernism was trendy; in the 1980s, it was mainstream. In the 1990s, it became institutionalized in higher education.

Attacks on Science

Science should be immune from postmodernist attacks because of its relationship with empirical data, which is the foundation of its disciplines. Data resulting from experiments must be considered the truth, or science cannot operate. It was surprising then when the postmodernists began an attack on science during the 1990s. Those attacks ushered in a period known as the Science Wars, which saw many postmodernists attempting to reinterpret science through the point of view of the scientist rather than the discipline. They began looking for bias in science based on gender, sexual orientation, class, and race. Claims were made that science was socially constructed because scientists were influenced by their material and spiritual needs, much like the acceptance of religion. Responding to these attacks, Paul R. Gross, Norman Levitt (1943-2009), and Martin Lewis (1957-) argued for the foundations of traditional science in their book *The Flight from Science and Reason* (1996). They accused the postmodernists of using politics to attack science, which they did not understand. During the 1990s, attempts were made to mediate the differences between science and postmodernism to find common ground. These efforts produced a standoff rather than a reconciliation, and eventually, the postmodernists abandoned their efforts to radicalize science.

Non-Traditional Areas of Study
Non-traditional disciplines were introduced to American universities in the late 1960s, responding to demands for a focus on the problems of identity groups. The first of these disciplines was Women's Studies (1969). That discipline sought to examine issues unique to women and how those issues were reflections of societal structure.

Academic disciplines were created for the first time without connecting to another domain. From the time of the Enlightenment, when academic disciplines began to be formally organized, new disciplines were created by partitioning existing fields of study. When a discipline, such as psychology, became sufficiently complex, a new sub-discipline was created. Behavioral and Social Psychology was developed out of general psychology. Chemistry was a single discipline until the need arose for further specialization, which led to the creation of Biochemistry and Physical Chemistry.

Women's studies and similar disciplines, such as Gender and Afro-American studies, did not evolve from a historical model. These are the names of political grievances, not disciplines.[20] Their sole purpose was to fight for the advancement of disadvantaged groups. There is no question that the initial premises of these disciplines is valid; their

---

[20] Roger Kimball. *Tenured Radicals*. Page xv.

members have been deprived. There is no question that these groups need advocates to act on their behalf. But the concept behind these groups' creation has corrupted their programs' objectives.

Unlike established disciplines, these new disciplines do not focus on a balanced debate. Injustices from the past are not put into the context of the times, and no focus is placed on the progress made in mitigating them. Their approach has become radicalized and politicized, neatly fitting into the radical left's playbook. As stated in socialist theory, condemning the past justifies discarding it.

Research Censorship

Recently, the impact of left ideas on university faculty members has been significant and threatens the fundamental character of scholarly research. Left-leaning faculty and administrators have embraced identity issues and used them to censor any point of view that differs from their dogmatic position. This dogma applies to what professors can say and what kind of research they do.

For example, radical Feminists advance the idea that gender is culturally constructed, consistent with postmodernist views. Researchers who produce data showing that men and women are different are now attacked and accused of discrimination. Gone are the days when faculty members could freely express themselves, no matter how controversial the topic. With opposing views suppressed, universities operate as echo chambers of left political ideology. Professors are reluctant to discuss their research results when they counter the prevailing ideology.

How ironic that the generation that fought for free speech in the 1960s wants to deny that right to the current generation.

Mike Adams was a criminology professor at the University of North Carolina at Wilmington. An outspoken conservative, Adams was the subject of a campaign to get him fired. In June 2020, two petitions on Change.org pressured the school to fire him. An open letter signed by hundreds of criminology professors and graduate students around the country criticized Adams for what they perceived as hate speech.[21]

Gregory Manco had been a non-tenured assistant math professor and volunteer assistant baseball coach at St. Joseph's University in Philadelphia, starting in 2005. In February 2021, Manco tweeted via an anonymous account critical of reparations for slavery and racial-sensitivity training. A St. Joseph's student recognized the account was Manco's and reported it to administrators, leading the school to launch an external investigation and put him on paid leave indefinitely.[22]

---

[21] Shibley, Robert. *In Memorium*, Professor Mike Adams. Fire Magazine, August 1, 2020

[22] Change.org. Support and Save Dr. Greg Manco of Saint Joseph's University from Cancel Culture. https://www.change.org/p/saint-joseph-s-university-support-and-save-dr-greg-manco-of-saint-joseph-s-university-from-cancel-culture

John Staddon, a Professor Emeritus of Psychology and Neuroscience at Duke University, was removed from the American Psychological Association's email discussion group after commenting that there were only two sexes.[23]

A former psychology professor at the University of Central Florida, Charles Negy, was fired after 22 years of service for criticizing the idea of systemic racism and white privilege.[24]

These are a few examples where public statements by academics, opposed to left dogma led to their censure or expulsion.

Balance of Views
One need only examine the distribution of political views among today's faculty to demonstrate how left ideology controls university faculty at elite institutions.

Below is a list of disciplines showing the ratio of liberal to conservative faculty members in that discipline.

Engineering	1.6 to 1
Chemistry	5 to 1
Physics	6 to 1

---

[23] Neuroscience Professor Removed from APA Discussion After Saying There Are Only Two Sexes. Newsweek, May 14, 2021

[24] UCF professor fired following controversial tweets about 'Black privilege' has job reinstated. New York Times, May 19, 2022.

Political Science	8 to 1
Psychology	16 to 1
Biology	20 to 1
Environmental	35 to 1
Art	40 to 1
Sociology	43 to 1
Anthropology	no conservatives in the sample
Communications	no conservatives in the sample[25]

The liberal-to-conservative faculty ratio averages 5 or 6 to 1 in the sciences. In the social sciences and humanities, the balance starts at 16 to 1 and grows until we reach disciplines like communications and anthropology, which had no conservative professors in the sample.

Today, conservative research in the social sciences has been relegated to think tanks funded by conservatives who support those points of view. That research receives limited public exposure because the left media censor it.

Students
In the past, universities were institutions where young people received preparation for life in the real world. Students select a field of study and develop deep knowledge in that subject to create the foundation for a successful career. Along the way, they were challenged by exposure to opposing and controversial points of view to help them seek the truth for themselves.

---

[25] M Langbert. 2018. "*Homogeneity: The Political Affiliations of Elite Liberal Arts College Faculty*." Academic Questions 31:2.

Before the 1960s, universities served as babysitters for college students whose parents expected them to be protected.[26] The counterculture movement swept away that model when students reacted against American society and its support of the Vietnam War. Today, life in the university is the opposite. Students are encouraged by faculty to accept a liberal ideology that is opposed to conservatism. Students are indoctrinated in identity politics and postmodernism, which focuses on the evil of inequality and privilege. They protest against conservative speakers and shut down free speech, saying, "You have no right to speak. You're a white male," "As a person in a position of power. Your statements are suspect because your goal is to protect that power," or "The statistics you present are questionable because they contradict information. I was told is true."

For many students, postmodernism was their primary exposure to critical thought. They are not exposed to alternative philosophies and must be shown papers critical of postmodernist principles. That means the brightest of the middle and upper classes are being indoctrinated in a mode of discourse that is relativistic and skeptical. Many students are attracted by postmodernism's playfulness and lack of respect for tradition. They come away believing they are involved in a significant movement when, in fact, they are being brainwashed using a tool that misrepresents reality. Postmodernism is not an ideology; it's a system of criticism

---

[26] P. Lee. *The curious life of in loco parentis in American universities*. Higher Education in Review, 8, 65-90.

that discredits traditional ideas. It offers nothing to replace what it attempts to tear down.

The left has a willing audience when it touts its ideology because college-age students are transitioning from parental control and willingly reject the establishment and its traditions. To them, socialism is more attractive than capitalism because it purports to help the disadvantaged instead of exploiting them. Students accept this assertion because they don't know history. When interviewed on the street, students can't answer simple civics questions about our government, so how can they accurately evaluate political systems?

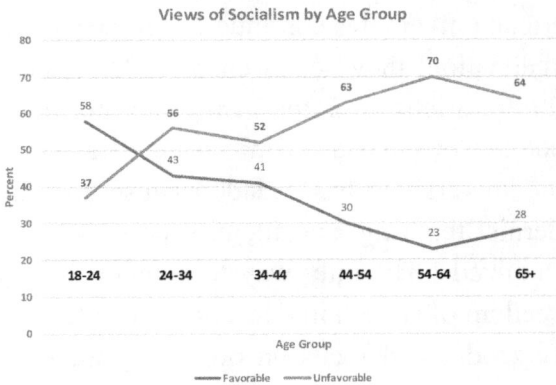

Views of Socialism by Age Group

Age Group	Favorable	Unfavorable
18-24	58	37
24-34	56	43
34-44	52	41
44-54	63	30
54-64	70	23
65+	64	28

College-age young people are the only group that believes socialism is superior to capitalism. When students graduate and begin understanding how the economy functions, they see the truth about capitalism (good and bad) and why it's superior to socialism. The chart above was taken from a recently released survey from The Federalist.[27]

Of course, not all students are progressives or liberals. An equal number are conservative, and these students are less susceptible to coercion from the left. Unfortunately, conservative students are afraid to speak out for fear of backlash. In 2021, the Foundation for Individual Rights in Education (FIRE) published a free speech survey assembled from questionnaires filled out by college students. A poll of nearly 20,000 students on 55 campuses survey found that 6 out of 10 felt they could not express an opinion for fear of adverse reactions from peers, faculty, or administrators.[28]

The Future of Academia
As American universities continue down the path of politics and radicalization, they act as enablers for attacks against American traditions and the American political system. Hope that the original academic principles will return to American universities has faded because socialist views, postmodernist thinking, and identity politics have become institutionalized. The only way to counter this trend is to revive freedom of speech in educational institutions without political agendas and focus on providing students with an ideologically balanced education.

---

[27] Emily Ekins and Joy Pullman. *Why So Many Millennials Are Socialists*. Cato Institute. February 15, 2016.

[28] *2021 College Free Speech Rankings*. Free Speech for Individual Rights in Education (FIRE), September 21, 2021.

CHAPTER EIGHT

MAINSTREAM MEDIA MOVES TO THE LEFT

The mainstream media has its agenda. They do not want to print the facts. They have an agenda, they have a slant, they have a bias. It is outrageous to me. **Curt Weldon**

Newspapers appeared in America after permanent colonial settlements were established in the early 17th Century. Most went out of business before the first successful newspaper, The Boston News-Letter, was founded in Boston in 1704. Its primary purpose was to disseminate information about local businesses and print advertisements, supporting the paper's cost. Benjamin Franklin became a newspaperman after purchasing *The Gazette* in 1729. Franklin expanded the content of his writing, adding regular articles he composed. The report featured travel stories and news from foreign countries, employment notices, and items lost and found. By the time Franklin gave control of the paper to his partner in 1748, the Gazette had become one of the most popular newspapers in the colonies.

As the American Revolution approached, colonial newspapers became more political. They were fiercely loyal to the colonial cause and quick to attack every British attempt at exploitation. There were 37 newspapers in America when the revolution began, but only six more were added during the conflict because money and supplies were difficult to obtain.

After the Constitution was ratified in 1788 and soon after the election of George Washington (1732-1799) as the first American president, political factions with opposing views began to make themselves heard. Throughout the Constitution period, there was severe disagreement, among the founders, regarding the distribution of power in the federal government. Still, those disagreements were put aside to get an agreement on the final document. Once the government began to operate, those disagreements resurfaced. On one side stood the federalists, who believed a strong central government was needed to eliminate the defects of the Articles of Confederation. On the other side were the Republicans, who sought to limit the federal government's powers in favor of the power of the states. Each view had a representative in Washington's cabinet. Secretary of the Treasury Alexander Hamilton (1757-1804) carried the banner for the Federalists, while Secretary of State Thomas Jefferson (1743-1826, represented Republican interests. Jefferson and Hamilton could not resolve their differences, and when neither man could influence Wahington in their direction, both resigned from the cabinet. Both started a propaganda campaign by investing in newspapers that agreed to print stories supporting their political positions. Jefferson eventually won the publicity battle because Americans preferred democracy over a monarchy and refused to vote for a strong central government. Federalist power began to fade after President John Adams (1735-1826) was defeated by Jefferson in the 1800 presidential election.

Newspapers became more partisan after 1800, as the public demanded articles that matched their political views. The people believed complimentary newspapers were the right of citizens and often refused to pay subscription fees. Publishers tolerated the loss of revenue because expanding subscription lists allowed them to raise the price of advertising.

The demise of the Federalists ushered in an *Era of Good Feelings* under the administration of James Monroe (1817-1825). It was a time when the Democratic-Republicans, the party of Thomas Jefferson, dominated national politics with little or no opposition. That political peace was broken in the late 1820s as controversies over slavery, commerce, and economics began to divide the nation. The Democratic-Republicans split, forming the Democratic and Republican Parties. The Democrats favored states' rights and a strong presidency. The Republicans, who eventually became the Whig Party, favored Congressional dominance and a weak president. Newspapers responded to the new political environment by aligning themselves with one of the parties. During that decade, for the first time, correspondents from newspapers outside the nation's capital were sent to Washington to report on the activities of the Federal Government.

In the years before the Civil War, improvements in newspaper printing allowed publishers to achieve high circulation and increase revenue while keeping costs under control. The development of photography and the invention of the telegraph enhanced the practice of journalism. Although photographs could only be reproduced in newspapers and magazines in the late 19th Century, they were often used as models for illustrations accompanying news stories.

The Civil War period saw the advent of newspaper war correspondence. The telegraph in the field permitted correspondents to file reports with their papers in a matter of hours rather than days or weeks. Unfortunately, the rapid transmission of information created security problems for civil and military authorities, so messages were often censored.

In the late 19th Century, access to inexpensive newspapers expanded readership exponentially. Many cities had competing newspapers, each supporting a different political party. The separation of news from editorials partially mitigated bias. Editorials often accompanied cartoons, which poked fun at the publishers' opponents.

In the 1890s, a few high-profile metropolitan newspapers began using a yellow journalism reporting style. This term was applied to American newspapers that replaced well-researched news with sensational headlines to increase readership. The leaders of this new style were William Randolph Hearst in New York City and Joseph Pulitzer in

St. Louis. In 1898, Hearst falsified or exaggerated sensational stories about atrocities in Cuba and the sinking of the USS Maine to boost circulation. Pulitzer claimed his approach was adopted to print stories the commoner wanted to read for humanitarian reasons. In the 1890s, yellow Journalism spread across the country and became the new philosophy for newspaper publishing.

Characteristics that had previously distinguished one newspaper from another began to disappear early in the 20th Century as increasing numbers of papers started to rely on wire services and syndicates for news from distant places. These news suppliers adopted a straightforward, objective reporting style to service clients at both ends of the political spectrum. However, the opinions expressed by the newspapers on their editorial pages continued to reflect their publisher's political opinions.

The entrance of radio into the news business after 1920 and television after the Second World War forced newspapers to redefine their relationship with the news. The motion picture newsreel allowed the American public to see and hear about the news. Critics of these new media forms accused them of exploiting freedom from regulation to make money instead of fulfilling their vital role as independent sources of information. The press had always been urged to be socially responsible and was supposed to use its freedom to report important news to a decision-making electorate instead of providing entertainment.

Donald Trump wasn't the only president with stormy press relations. President Roosevelt went to war with the newspaper publishers during the New Deal period over his Depression Era programs. Three years after Roosevelt's election, after a honeymoon period of cooperation, Roosevelt became frustrated with his press coverage. During the 1936 election campaign, he claimed that 85% of newspapers were against him.[29] To gain more control of his message, Roosevelt sidestepped the press and used his "fireside chat" radio broadcasts to speak directly to the American people. He intended these talks to explain federal government policy and the reasons behind his political positions. Roosevelt also employed censorship, using the FCC (Federal Communications Commission) to block articles and broadcasts deemed "harmful" to his administration.

The press did not cover the problems experienced by minority groups until they surfaced during the Civil Rights Movement. Conservative newspapers strongly slanted news about Civil Rights, blaming the unrest on Southern blacks or communists. In some cases, Southern television stations refused to air programs such as *I Spy* and *Star Trek* because of their racially-mixed casts. Newspapers supporting civil rights, labor unions, and liberal social reform were often accused of pro-communist bias.

During the last decades of the 20th Century, television news broadcasts replaced newspapers as the nation's primary

---

[29] Dave Beito. *FDR's War Against the Press*. Reason Magazine, May 2017.

news source. This development caused hundreds of newspapers to go out of business. As they worked to increase efficiency, broadcast media companies consolidated through mergers, intending to create a larger market share for themselves.

News in the 21st Century
The broadcast media dominate the news in the 21st Century through television and the internet. Both mirror the tribalism that emerged in the United States in the 1990s. Media outlets have gravitated toward one side of the political spectrum or the other, sensing that an ideological bias benefits them. A Pew study from 2021 illustrates the current media polarization. Pew selected 30 news sources covering the spectrum of political views from liberal to conservative. Pew asked for viewers' opinions regarding their trust level in each. Democratic voters *trusted* twenty-two of those sources, while Republican voters *distrusted* twenty.[30]

The problem with politicizing the media is that many news sources lean left over right. If we look at the evening news market share, the three mainstream networks (ABC, NBC, and CBS) dwarf the number of viewers on cable networks. The big three have about 17 million viewers per half-hour evening news broadcast, while the popular cable news networks have about 5 million viewers for the entire prime-time period. The following chart depicts the level of political bias for the mainstream and cable networks. This data is

---

[30] U.S. Media Polarization and the 2020 Election: *A Nation Divided*. Pew Research Center, January 24, 2020.

compiled continuously by AllSides.com based on viewer surveys.

If we apply the audience figures to the chart above, the results show that 8% of the evening news presents right-leaning content, while 92% presents left-leaning stories. Since fewer sources of conservative (or independent) news content exist, liberals have greater power to influence the public.

An October 2017 Pew Research report found that 62% of stories involving U.S. Republican President Donald Trump had negative assessments during his first 60 days in office, compared to only 5% of accounts with a positive evaluation. By comparison, the study found that Democratic President Barack Obama received far more favorable coverage in his first 60 days in office; Obama was identified as positive in 42% of stories during that period, and only 20% were as unfavorable.[31]

A May 2017 study from Harvard University's Kennedy School's Shorenstein Center on Media, Politics, and Public identified a similar negative tone in coverage during Trump's first 100 days in office. That study found that 93% of CNN and NBC coverage of President Trump during the period was negative. It also found that 91% of CBS coverage was negative, and 87% of New York Times coverage was negative during Trump's first 100 days.[32]

An October 2018 Rasmussen Reports poll of 1,000 likely voters found that 45% of Americans believed that when reporters wrote about a congressional race, they were trying to help the Democratic candidate. Alternatively, only 11% believed most reporters aimed to support Republican candidates.[33]

---

[31] Pew Research. *Covering President Trump in a Polarized Media Environment*. October 2, 2017.

[32] Shorenstein Center on Media, Politics and Public Policy. *News Coverage of Donald Trump's First 100 Days*. May 18, 2017.

[33] Rasmussen Reports. *Voters Think Reporters Trying to Help Democrats in Midterm Elections*. Thursday, October 25, 2018.

Respect for the Mainstream Media

A 1956 American National Election Study found that 66% of Americans thought newspapers were fair, including 78% of Republicans and 64% of Democrats. In the years since then, the level of confidence has decreased dramatically.

Gallup Polls since 1997 have shown that most Americans do not have confidence in the mass media reporting accurately and fairly. According to Gallup, the American public's trust has generally declined in the first two decades of the 21st Century.

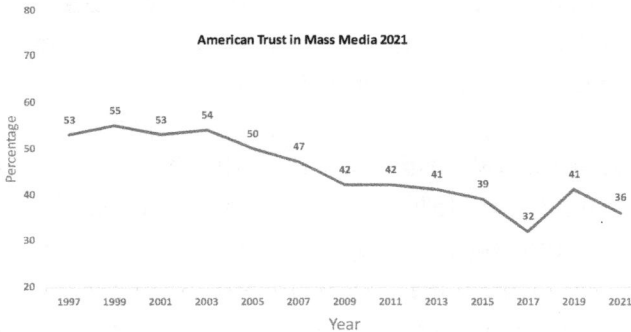

American Trust in Mass Media 2021

Today, trust in the media is 33% lower than in 1997[34] Politicization, which began in the mid-1990s, contributed to the decline. Since the press abandoned objectivity, large groups on each side of the political spectrum disagree with the reporting. There was a significant increase in liberal trust after Trump was elected. The dominance of the left-leaning

---

[34] Gallup. *Americans' Trust in Media Dips to Second Lowest on Record.* October 7, 2021.

media caused that increase, their coverage of Trump as an adversary and liberal reliance on them as reporting the truth.

Americans Trust in Mass Media by Party

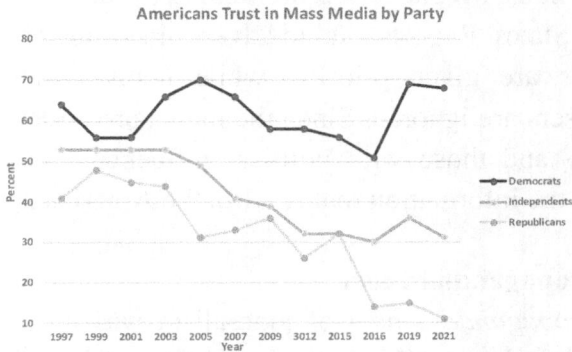

The jump in liberal confidence can be seen clearly after 2016. There was also a corresponding drop in conservative trust based on a perceived liberal bias against Trump. That trust factor did not rebound following Biden's election, demonstrating a continuation of the tribal view of media content. Independent voters, who are not typically associated with a party, have lost trust in the media, dropping from 52% in 1997 to 30% in 2021.

Corporate Control
Five corporate conglomerates (AT&T, Comcast, Disney, Fox Corporation, and Viacom/CBS) own the majority of mass media outlets in the United States. The Telecommunications Act of 1996 enabled this consolidation. That act deregulated cable television service, allowing local

telephone companies to provide cable television service, and increased the number of television stations a single corporation could own. Broad corporate ownership means their media may suppress stories that are critical of these corporations. Media outlets are funded by advertising in the United States. Reports vital to advertisers or the advertiser's interests are given priority, while items criticizing the advertisers are ignored. Since the media are directed by the wealthy and those with political influence, those groups control the information that reaches the American public.

The Propaganda Model

The *Propaganda Model* of journalism was introduced by Edward S. Herman (1925-2017) and Noam Chomsky (1928) in the late 1990s. The model seeks to explain how populations are manipulated and how consent for economic, social, and political policies, both foreign and domestic, is manufactured in the public mind by journalists. The theory asserts that corporate media structure (e.g., through advertising, the concentration of media ownership, or government sourcing) creates an inherent conflict of interest and acts as propaganda for specific political groups.

The propaganda model calls out self-censorship, as a factor, in the corporate system. Reporters, especially editors, share or acquire values that agree with corporate elites to further their careers. Those who do not are marginalized or fired. The model identifies the relationship between those funding media sources and media coverage. A strong link likely means a conflict of interest.

Herman and Chomsky argued that comparing journalists' voting records to their media employers is wrong. They concede that media owners and newsmakers have an agenda subordinated to corporate interests. Some critics accuse media sources of focusing on good news and ignoring the real problems in society. Before the Great Recession (2008), corporate influence tended to the right. Since then, the profit-making incentive of the American media led them to seek an uncontroversial position, representing the largest possible audience. Since the pandemic, however, following the advent of corporate *wokeism*, significant businesses in the United States have moved to the left.

Infotainment
Media profits depend on viewership numbers rather than the quality of the programming. According to some, the profit-driven quest for high numbers of viewers, rather than high quality for viewers, has resulted in a transition from legitimate news and analysis to entertainment, sometimes called *infotainment*. Imitating the rhythm of sports reports, exciting live coverage of major political crises and foreign wars is now available for viewers 24 hours a day.

View of Journalists
Journalists in the United States differ markedly from the general public in their views of *bothsidesism* – whether journalists should always strive to give equal coverage to all sides of an issue – according to a recent Pew Research Center study.

U.S. journalists more likely than the public to say all sides don't always deserve equal coverage

% who say ...

	Journalists should always strive to give every side equal coverage	Every side does not always deserve equal coverage
U.S. journalists	44%	55%
U.S. adults	76	22

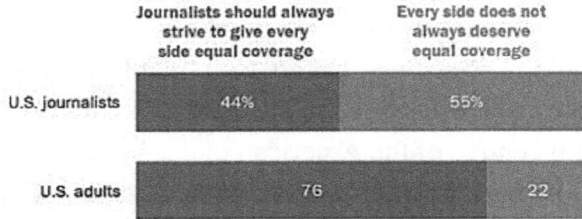

Note: Respondents who did not answer not shown.
Source: Survey of U.S. journalists conducted Feb. 16-March 17, 2022. Survey of U.S. adults conducted Feb. 7-13, 2022.

PEW RESEARCH CENTER

According to a recent Pew Research Center study, more than half of the journalists surveyed (55%) say that each side does not always deserve equal coverage in the news. While 22% of Americans agree, 76% say journalists should always strive to give all sides the same analysis.

According to a study by Lars Willnat and David H. Weaver, professors of Journalism at Indiana University, who conducted online interviews with 1,080 reporters between August and December 2013, 28.1% of U.S. journalists identify as liberals, 7.1% as conservatives, and 50.2% as Independents.[35] Additionally, a 2018 Arizona State University and Texas A & M University study of 462

---

[35] Lars Willnat and David Weaver. *The American Journalist in The Digital Age (PDF)*. Indiana University. May 2014.

financial journalists found that there were 13 times the number of financial journalists who identified as liberal as opposed to those who identified as conservative.[36]

The Future of Mass Media
Newspapers have been a critical component of America's communication infrastructure since the United States was founded. They have always given Americans access to what is new and validated the truth presented by the nation's institutions. During the 20th Century, television became the dominant news source, replacing print media. Large corporations control broadcast news to publicize their political positions. Those companies have been moving to the left because they find it practical to employ left ideology. Schools of journalism reinforce this left-leaning philosophy by turning out left-leaning graduates.

People want to listen to outlets that support their political positions, so the media became tribal as American society began to splinter. Controversial political positions strengthen tribalism by creating an echo chamber inside each tribe that resists moderation. Each tribe is bombarded with the same ideas and stories, repeatedly reinforcing their beliefs. Media bias affects all Americans and acts as a force against any effort to unify politics in the United States.

---

[36] Investor's Business Daily. *Media Bias: Pretty Much All of Journalism Now Leans Left, Study Shows.* November 16, 2018.

CHAPTER NINE

SOCIAL MEDIA LEANS LEFT

The goal of social media is to turn customers into a volunteer marketing army. **Jay Baer**

Social media has profoundly impacted American society since it was established in the early 2000s. It wouldn't be hyperbole to say its impact has been more significant than any communication form in human history because humans have never experienced a communication system that was universal, immediate, and unfiltered.

Social media was envisioned with the noblest intentions, to act as an equalizing force to give a voice to those lacking one and act as a change agent to improve people's lives. Censorship should not be employed to stop the expression and discussion of ideas in the ideal implementation of this media. Unfortunately, individuals and groups with sinister purposes compromised this lofty goal and have taken advantage of the openness. As a result, propaganda, fake news, and conspiracy theories have proliferated.

Social media companies lean left because they are California-based tech companies representing California values. They think of themselves as engines of information and information control. They believe they are performing a public service while making enormous profits by providing platforms that people can consume to their benefit. Those platforms come with unique problems, the most important of which is how the providers can apply controls to prevent harm while maintaining openness.

They think of themselves as engines of information and information control. They believe they are performing a public service while making enormous profits by informing the public. While this medium is unique in human history, it comes with particular problems, the most important of which is how to apply controls best to prevent harm while maintaining themselves as open platforms.

Social Media Emerges

The *Friendster* website was launched in 2003, starting the social network revolution. That new way of communicating caught on quickly and boasted of a community of three million users after its first year. Technological advances have opened the door for a unique and immediate means of human communication. In 2004, Mark Zuckerberg and some of his Harvard classmates created a site called *thefacebook.com*, which surpassed its competitors to become one of the world's most influential and successful social media platforms. As of July 2022, Facebook had over 2.9 billion active users. The Facebook format provides users with a personal page to post information on, which can be used to communicate with friends.

Twitter, founded in 2006, is a social media network designed to accommodate short conversations. Users can create a message containing up to 280 characters and post the text publicly. Twitter features *hashtags*, or labels, which identify groups and topics of interest to the user. As of 2022, Twitter had 450 million active users, including politicians, information agencies, companies, and individuals.

The success of Twitter and Facebook produced a flood of new social media products, vying for a piece of the market. *YouTube (now owned by Google), Instagram (now owned by Facebook), Snapchat, and TikTok* are significant players who have survived the competition by offering users a feature-rich platform. All these players owe their success to the invention of the smartphone.

The Mobile Revolution
The first mobile phone with internet connectivity was the Nokia 9000 Communicator, which appeared in 1996. NTT DoCoMo, in Japan, launched the first mobile Internet service in 1999. In these early years, internet phones had limited use because no applications operated on a cell phone.

The initial growth of mobile phone services occurred primarily in Asia as Japan, South Korea, and Taiwan quickly saw most internet users choosing internet connectivity by phone rather than computer. Many countries followed Asia in expanding internet access, including third-world countries lacking a landline telephone infrastructure. Mobile access accelerated in the United States following the first-generation iPhone launch on January 9, 2007. Less than one year later, mobile phones became the most popular internet access device. Americans were experiencing a new kind of freedom, communicating from anywhere, with a camera in their hand, and shopping without going to the store.

The expansion of smartphones, with internet access, forced companies to modify their applications to run on mobile devices. At the beginning of 2021, more than 4.8 billion people were using social media. Of those, 4.4 billion users accessed social media via a mobile phone.

Growth of Social Networking

For the last few years, companies like *Facebook, Twitter,* and *Google* have expanded their platforms or invested in new ones. The social media landscape has broadened from addressing local environments to reaching worldwide. Broadening their user communities has allowed platform providers to gain influence as advertising and marketing companies. They have added shopping functions to their platforms to increase the convenience for shoppers, which further increases their reach in the marketplace.

Once social media platforms reached significant viewer numbers, their audience size and changing usage patterns made them a desirable communication channel for business. Advertisers saw easy access and global reach as opportunities to make money. Marketing professionals and advertising agencies began to give social media priority for their promotional campaigns.

Apart from its commercial value, social media has become a conduit for mobilizing support, passing important information to the public, and reporting on government activities. Governments and non-government influencers have been actively using social media to influence their target audiences' knowledge, opinions, and behaviors.

News on social media
News broadcasts on social media become controversial if some deem the information inaccurate or fake. Easy access to social media and anonymity are a dangerous mix when it comes to ascertaining the truth. In the traditional media, journalists are trained to find the truth in a story by obtaining corroborating information. Editors check journalists to ensure a news item meets standards for accuracy and reliability. On social media, user credentials are not required.

Social media is often criticized for excessive influence over the news because its subscriber lists are significantly higher than other media forms. Since those platforms have a more significant impact, their responsibility to remove low-quality information is more elevated.

In 2016, according to Gottfried and Shearer, 62% of American adults received news on social media, with Facebook being the most popular conduit. An article published in 2017 in *The Journal of Economic Perspectives* discusses fake news and the public's response to it during the 2016 election. The results were obtained by analyzing browsing data, archives of fact-checking websites, and data from an online survey. The analysis indicated that social media was an essential but not dominant source of election news, with 14 percent of Americans calling it their "most important" source. The average American adult saw one or more fake news stories in the months before the election, with just over half of those who recalled seeing them believing them believed them. People were likelier to believe stories that favored their preferred candidate if they used ideologically segregated social media networks.

Social Media Content Moderation
Facebook, Twitter, and YouTube have evolved content moderation models in response to pressure from the American public and the government. All content was permitted at the time these platforms were launched. That openness was mandated through the federal government, prohibiting those sites from acting as *publishers;* they could only act as platforms for disseminating information.

That mandate quickly proved unworkable in practice because of the overwhelming quantity of material posted on the platforms. Facebook receives 510,000 comments per minute, for example. Protecting the public from hate speech, intimidation, violence, sex, and lies has proven challenging for social media companies. Their approach uses a combination of technology tools with human intervention to moderate content. Using technology requires categorizing the content to identify potential harm more easily. Categorization takes place through word scans that look for trigger words. Texts are analyzed semantically for meaning and intent. No system can identify all the content that needs to be blocked.

Technology limitations are not the whole story, however. Social media companies are profit-making ventures that rely on advertising revenue. They lose revenue if they employ content mediating tools that drive users off their platforms. More importantly, there is advertising value in controversy. Posts that are politically charged and stimulate user responses create interest and engagement. Those reasons act as motivators to limit content moderation.

Politics on social media
It was inevitable that social media would become politicized, following the path of every other institution, with influence, in America. Politicization has taken many forms, on these platforms, such as candidates posting information about themselves or against their opponents or advocates and surrogates posting in favor of candidates. Lying or misrepresenting a candidate's position is expected. Often, postings address controversial issues such as abortion, designed to inflame the rhetoric from one side or the other. The echo chamber serves both parties' tribal behavior. One needs only follow a group or individual that matches the individual's beliefs to receive support for their personal beliefs.

With politicization comes polarization, as the intensifying rhetoric plays into the tribalism epidemic that has infected all Americans. Social media companies maintain they do not fuel polarization, but several studies have shown they do.

> Our central conclusion, based on a review of more than 50 social science studies and interviews with more than 40 academics, policy experts, activists, and current and former industry people, is that platforms like Facebook, YouTube, and Twitter likely are not the root causes of political polarization, but they do exacerbate it.[37]

There is another way social media companies engage in politics. They spend their money to support candidates and issues at election time. Following is a list of large Silicon technology companies and the dollars spent on each political party during the first half of 2020.

Netflix   Democrats $340,485 (98%), Republicans - $7,124 (2%)
IBM   Democrats $1,496,234 (90%), Republicans - $163,804 (10%)
Google   Democrats $5,437,048 (88%), Republicans - $766,920 (12%)
Microsoft Democrats $3,969,072 (85%), Republicans - $690,953 (15%)
Apple   Democrats $1,243,825 (84%), Republicans - $228,653 (16%)
Amazon   Democrats $2,677,112 (77%), Republicans - $783,349 (23%)

These numbers show a solid commitment to the Democratic Party and a lack of interest in the Republican Party.

---

[37] Paul M. Barrett, Justin Hendrix, J. Grant Sims. *Fueling the Fire: How Social Media Intensifies U.S. Political Polarization - And What Can Be Done About It.* NYU Stern Center for Business and Human Rights, September, 2021.

Questionable Business Practices

Facebook, Twitter, and Google were accused of questionable business practices, including internet privacy violations, user information exploitation, and unfair business practices. Facebook allegedly produces damaging psychological effects on its users, including fear, shaming by others, intimidation, and addiction.[38]

All the key players have been criticized for allowing users to publish illegal or offensive material. Specifics include copyright infringement, hate speech, terrorism, fake news, crimes, murders, and live-streaming violent incidents. Facebook removed 3 billion fake accounts during the last quarter of 2018 and the first quarter of 2019.[39]

Political Censorship

The political right for censorship has attacked social media platforms. The accusations highlighted the censoring of political figures like Donald Trump. Conservatives created posts that were censored as untruthful.

---

[38] Settanni, Michele; Marengo, Davide; Fabris, Matteo Angelo; Longobardi, Claudio (2018). *"The interplay between ADHD symptoms and time perspective in addictive social media use: A study of adolescent Facebook users"*. Children and Youth Services Review. Elsevier. **89**:165170. doi:10.1016/j.childyouth. 2018.04.031. S2CID 149795392.

[39] Sullivan, Mark *Facebook catches 3 billion fake accounts, but the ones it misses are the real problem*. Fast Company, May 23, 2019

Here are a few examples.

During the pandemic, conservative posts that advocated the consideration of therapeutics showing promise in treating the disease (Ivermectin) were removed and labeled as untruthful. Ivermectin was later revealed to be a useful therapeutic and is in use today.

Social media platforms chose to mimic the policies of the CDC in the letter. Ideas were censored if they varied from CDC guidelines. Two emergency doctors from Los Angeles had their YouTube video taken down because they questioned whether lockdowns were effective. Any posts suggesting the vaccines were being rushed into use were censored, including those implying the vaccines were inadequately tested on pregnant women. The federal government (Biden administration) felt compelled to protect the profits of their partner pharmaceutical companies as part of the deal to manufacture the vaccines.

The Biden administration was colluding with social media companies to censor conservative views. According to Missouri Attorney General Eric Schmitt, the Republican nominee for U.S. Senate. Schmitt released emails that indicate collaboration between President Biden's executive branch and Silicon Valley to censor Americans online. The emails show that more than 45 officials at various federal agencies and numerous White House staffers were in regular conversation with social media companies about removing "undesirable" content from their platforms—content coming from the administration's political opposition.[40]

Conservatives pushed the Hunter Biden laptop controversy on social media. These posts were blocked as lies and disinformation by former Twitter employees who admitted that the New York Post's Hunter Biden laptop story didn't violate any Twitter policies but was taken down anyway. The employees later admitted they did not attempt to verify the authenticity of the Hunter Biden laptop story.

Public Opinion
According to a 2020 survey by the Pew Research Center, Americans believed social media was biased toward the left. Although the fact that 90% of Republicans view social media as discriminatory should not be surprising, 73% of Americans believe that social media sites censor content with which they disagree. The survey found the public evenly split on whether social media companies should engage in fact-checking. Still, there is little public confidence the platforms can accurately determine which content should be flagged.

Reflecting the difference in the two groups on political morality, most Democrats say they strongly or somewhat approve of social media companies labeling inaccurate or misleading specific posts on their platforms. Most Republicans say they at least somewhat disapprove of this

[40] Jake Denton. *Biden Administration Outsourcing Online Censorship of Conservatives*. The Heritage Foundation. Commentary: Technology. October 14, 2022

practice. For the Democrats, the issue is equality; for the Republicans, the moral value is liberty and free speech. Republicans are far more likely than Democrats to say they have no confidence that social media companies can accurately determine which posts should be marked as inaccurate or misleading (50% vs. 11%).[41]

Government action against social media companies

The federal government in the regulation and control of social media companies has been growing recently, although the parties have different views of the problem. Republicans want to stop censorship of conservative ideas. They believe social media platforms exert too much influence in representing liberal issues. Democrats want to protect privacy and threats against teens and young children.

As of the summer of 2022, Congress was considering legislation to bring social media under its control. A bill to accomplish that purpose was introduced in Senate on May 18, 2021, called The Social Media Privacy Protection and Consumer Rights Act of 2021. It has not passed Congress as of mid-2023.

This bill requires online platform operators to inform users when their data will be collected and used by the media operator and third parties. The operator must provide the user an option to specify their privacy preferences. The operator must offer the user a copy of the user data the

---

[41] Emily A. Vogels, Andrew Perrin, and Monica Anderson. *Most Americans Think Social Media Sites Censor Political Viewpoints.* Pew Research Center, August 19, 2020.

operator has processed, free of charge and in an electronic format, and notify a user within 72 hours of becoming aware that the user's data has violated the security platform. Violating the bill's privacy requirements shall be considered an unfair or deceptive act or practice under the Federal Trade Commission Act. The Federal Trade Commission (FTC) may enforce this bill against common carriers regulated by the Federal Communications Commission under the Communications Act of 1934. Common carriers regulated under that Act are exempt from the FTC's enforcement authority.

A state may bring a civil action in federal court regarding such violations. Lawmakers in 34 red and blue states are considering legislation to control the way online companies handle users' content. More than 100 bills have been introduced between July 2021 and July 2022 to regulate how social media companies such as Facebook and Twitter manage users' posts. There are problems with this process, as one might imagine. Since the platforms are not operating within states but across the country, there is a question of whether states have the authority to regulate those platforms. Secondly, the government cannot control speech emulating from private companies if it is protected. There could be years of lawsuits attempting to define the critical first amendment issues that apply to social media platforms.

On January 11, 2023, the Biden administration issued a press release regarding social media. Its recommendations support most of what each party wants to see enacted. It reads, in part,

The risks Big Tech poses for ordinary Americans are clear. Big Tech companies collect huge amounts of data on the things we buy, on the websites we visit, on the places we go, and, most troubling of all, on our children. As I said last year in my State of the Union address, millions of young people are struggling with bullying, violence, trauma, and mental health. We must hold social-media companies accountable for the experiment they are running on our children for profit.

To keep Americans on their platforms, Big Tech companies often use users' data to direct them toward extreme and polarizing content that is likely to keep them logged on and clicking. All too often, tragic violence has been linked to toxic online echo chambers.

What's more, social media and other platforms have allowed abusive and even criminal conduct, like cyberstalking, child sexual exploitation, nonconsensual pornography, and the sale of dangerous drugs. In other cases, Big Tech companies have elbowed mom-and-pop businesses out of their platforms, disadvantaged them, or charged them outlandish prices, making it harder for them to compete and grow, and thereby stifling innovation.

First, we need serious federal protections for Americans' privacy. That means clear limits on how companies can collect, use, and share highly personal data—your internet history, your communications, your location, and your health, genetic and biometric data. It's not enough for companies to disclose what data they're collecting. Much of that data shouldn't be collected in the first place. These protections should be even stronger for young people, who are especially vulnerable online. We should limit targeted advertising and ban it altogether for children.

Second, we need Big Tech companies to take responsibility for the content they spread and the algorithms they use. That's why I've long said we must fundamentally reform Section 230 of the Communications Decency Act, which protects tech companies from legal responsibility for content posted on their sites. Third, we need to bring more competition back to the tech sector. My administration has made strong progress in promoting competition throughout the economy, consistent with my July 2021 executive order. [42]

---

[42] Joe Biden. *Republicans and Democrats, Unite Against Big Tech Abuses*
Congress can find common ground on the protection of privacy, competition, and American children. Press release, January 11, 2023.

That press release represents an opportunity for both parties to unite and establish control over the social media industry. In a time of great division in government, this bill could potentially satisfy both sides and, at the same time, accomplish something meaningful for the American people.

CHAPTER TEN

WOKE CORPORATIONS

Never think that corporations have our best interests in mind. Their morality is profitability. **Unknown**

Woke and wokeism are children of the second decade of the 21st century, gaining public attention after the Michael Brown shooting 2014. The word woke initially referred to issues of racial prejudice affecting African Americans, but later its use expanded to encompass all issues that constitute the left's culture war attack strategy. The Trump presidency exacerbated the situation with its "in your face" rudeness and tacit support of fringe groups on the Right.

Lately, wokeism has been focused on discrimination against African-Americans. This discrimination became manifest in ideas like the United States has never been a democracy, white people enjoy a special privilege, people of color suffer from systemic racism, law enforcement is designed to discriminate against people of color, capitalism is deeply flawed, and African-Americans deserve reparations for their mistreatment. Many of these ideas are unpopular across the United States, even among the centrists in the Democratic Party.

Woke ideology began to appear in corporate culture between the Great Recession and the pandemic. After decades of balancing their support between the parties, corporations were the last American institutions to become overtly political.

Corporate Wokeism

Vivek Ramaswamy's 2021 book *Woke, Inc* vividly describes Corporations as a platform for identity politics.[43] Ramaswamy had a front-row seat for the growth in corporate wokeism as an Ivy League student, employee at Goldman Sachs, and CEO of his own pharmaceutical company. The book skillfully describes the alliance between woke activists, the federal government, universities, and large corporations.

Corporations were attracted to wokeism because it offered a way to support important causes to the left. Since the left, through its cultural issues and reach, has the leverage to damage a business's reputation, corporations wanted to show they were on board with social justice and equality issues. CEOs also realized emphasizing social issues had a second benefit; it diverted the public's attention away from their bad behavior. When corporations engage in activities that hurt people, they look for ways to minimize the damage. They could offset that damage by loudly broadcasting their concern for social justice.

---

[43] Vivek Ramaswamy. *Woke, Inc. Inside Corporate America's Social Justice Scam.* Center Street Publishing, New York, 2021

Before discussing this topic further, it's essential to identify the differences between woke capitalism and wokeism outside corporate America because they differ. Outside corporate America, wokeism is ubiquitous, dominating the news and central to the battlefront of the culture wars.

Inside the corporate boardroom, the term stakeholder capitalism seeks to redefine the purpose of a corporation. Historically, corporations produced profits for their shareholders, who took a risk by investing in the company. Management makes decisions that will increase shareholder value. The left wants the corporate purpose redefined to include all "stakeholders" in the business, including employees, customers, and vendors. For example, there is pressure to put employees on the board of directors, who can push for changes that benefit the employees. Stakeholder capitalism also includes other left-agenda issues, such as the environment, women's issues, and diversity.

Most of the objectives of woke capitalism make sense because they are suitable for the country. Only foolish people would suggest that the environment and women's issues are unimportant. Because humanity represents the greatest danger to our planet, all possible means should be used to limit the damage caused by human consumption and waste. Women should have the same career choices as men. Decisions to hire or promote women should on their skills and experience, not their gender. Minorities should have equal opportunities for jobs and promotions like everyone else. Corporations should create policies to provide equal

137

consideration, not quotas. Corporations should treat their employees fairly by adhering to a code of conduct.

Despite the seemingly good intentions behind woke capitalism, its approach has two problems. The first problem is culture warriors are making the rules on the left rather than through a left-right consensus. Second, changing the corporate direction based on stakeholder capitalism represents a risk to the business. That risk damages corporate performance due to diverting attention to issues outside the company's operation.

The Managerial Class and Politics

Members of America's managerial class now use business and politics to increase their reputation and power. Historically, there was a dividing line between the politics of elites and the politics of the companies they ran. Elites addressed politics in their private lives and not in their business. Today, pursuing political agendas sits at the center of their business focus. Executives, who oversee a social justice agenda, discard the will of shareholders to seek power for themselves, and they substitute their self-serving judgments for the majority will of shareholders.

The purpose of a corporation cannot be realized when it's led by woke individuals rather than those who truly represent the essence of the business. A manufacturing company should focus on how to produce its product, meet a need in the marketplace, and enjoy the profits obtained from those efforts. A services company should focus on efficient service delivery to grow its business. Neither should be distracted by pursuing a woke agenda if it directs business operations away from efficiency. Stakeholder capitalism requires that corporations advance societal goals over and above the corporation's essential purpose.

Unless America changes course, it will take on the character of Western European countries where business executives collaborate with the government to chart their society's path. The problem with that approach is that it represents the best path forward for the wealthy and not everyone. A corporate government partnership ignores the interests of the middle and lower classes.

Christophe Guilluy, in his excellent book, *Twilight of the Elites* (2019),[44] discussed the social and cultural problems in France. There, the government lost the support of the working class through its arrogance and self-indulgence.

Over the last few decades, France has embraced globalism wholeheartedly. The power and impact of global markets now dominate the French economy, replacing a society founded on egalitarian ideals with a disjointed and polarized one. A patriotic publicity campaign had disguised this unprecedented social and cultural disruption, but now the truth has become apparent. The elite class is supported by members of society who either benefit from its focus on globalization or are protected against its adverse consequences.

---

[44] Christophe Guilluy. *Twilight of the Elites: Prosperity, the Periphery, and the Future of France.* New Have, Yale University Press. 2019.

The only option for the lower classes is to revolt against the elites and try and take back control of their lives. Globalism is the source of this problem because it takes no responsibility for the lives of working people. French citizens are left with insecurity, expanded settling of immigrants in their space, and isolation from the upper classes.

Whether France can successfully deal with this problem depends on whether the political class is willing to listen to the demands of the ordinary people and do something to help them. The government must stop suppressing criticism of the existing system and seriously consider their people's grievances. Fraternité is embedded in the psychology of the French people, and they expect their government to recognize that fact.

Since the 2010s, when political polarization in the United States began to accelerate, Wokeism moved from Academia into the corporate space. Today, the federal government behaves like the Western European countries, transferring political power from the legislature to the executive branch bureaucracy and from there to their corporate and transnational partners. Those partners are "bought off" for following the executive branch's agenda.

During the Progressive Era, America's principles powered the reformers to overcome the selfish efforts of the managerial class. In its place, America's corporate leaders have pretended to transform themselves from evil exploiters of workers to moral and ethical advocates.

Silicon Valley Corporations

Silicon Valley corporations play a unique role in the woke capitalism story. They are a united entity dedicated to the implementation of a progressive ideology. Their power is almost unlimited because their audience is more significant than any other media source, and there is no brake on their efforts. Silicon Valley's influence over the 2020 election was an overt effort to impose its leaders' values and beliefs on the election process, acting against democratic principles.

Conservatives see Silicon Valley media as a threat to free speech in America. New conservative media cannot challenge the size and reach of prominent social media companies cannot be questioned.

The Danger of Wokeism

When America became tribal at the turn of the 21st Century, the government shifted from the American people to the ideological war between the parties. Each party seeks to destroy the other by any means available. When either party gains control, the first thing they do is reverse the work of the previous party. Political groups have replaced America's national identity.

Pluralism is supposed to be the variation of identities WITHIN us. The woke identity concept ignores what's inside and defines us by physical characteristics (the OUTSIDE). The view of looking at people on the outside is created racism in the first place. Woke ideology celebrates a room full of people of different colors. That is the wrong view because the group in the room should reflect different philosophies, moral points of view, and political beliefs. An individual's contribution should be measured from the inside, not the outside.

The problem with wokeism in the corporate world is that it blurs the line between capitalism and politics. Making corporations into political groups allows them to unleash their power to persuade and control. It dilutes their function as instruments of capitalism.

Wokeism in Europe

French President Emmanuel Macron recently told Elle Magazine that woke culture, which he says is imported from the U.S., is racializing his country, and he denounced the ideology, along with other prominent French figures. Macron stated that the woke doctrine has been causing significant division among the minorities in his country. Surprisingly, in May 2023, Macron appointed a new education administrator, apparently a woke advocate.

The same criticism is seen throughout Europe. Postmodernism was never able to establish itself in Europe because philosophical ideas have well-established traditions that are not subject to faddishness. Yet postmodernism dominates academia in the United States. Will Europe be immune to Wokeism in the same way?

CHAPTER ELEVEN

THE ERODING OF AMERICAN TRADITIONS

No civilization would ever have been possible without a framework of stability to provide the wherein for the flux of change. Foremost among the stabilizing factors, more enduring than customs, manners, and traditions, are the legal systems that regulate our life in the world and our daily affairs with each other. **Hannah Arendt**

The subjects of contemporary social debate reflect the rapid change in American culture over the last several decades. That debate ignited culture wars in the 1970s and 1980s, pitting ideologues on the left against their opponents on the Right. Attacks against the status quo did not originate in the 1960s but began in the 1950s. The Vietnam War did not trigger this revolution; it had its genesis in the radical group of anti-establishment advocates known as the Beat Generation.

The Beat Generation
In 1948, Jack Kerouac (1922-1969) created the term Beat Generation to describe a specific non-conformist youth movement in post-World War II New York.

The word "Beat" describes individuals living a purposeful, non-conformist lifestyle. The term Beat was descriptive slang denoting the world of hustlers, drug addicts, and petty thieves that influenced the movement's founders, Allen Ginsberg (1926-1997) and Jack Kerouac (1922-1969). To Kerouac and Ginsberg, Beat was not just beaten down or downtrodden but had a spiritual aspect focused on opposition to the establishment.

As the Beat Generation grew, it became characterized as a generation of crazy, illuminated hipsters roaming America, serious, bumming, and hitchhiking everywhere, ragged but beautiful in an ugly but appealing way. This vision could describe Beat behavior on street corners in New York or a hundred other cities in postwar America. The Beats had intensity and conviction, and they lived as solitary outcasts.

The Beat philosophy opposed culture's trappings, including materialism and the desire to fit in. There was a religious-like element to their willingness to explore the inner self, relating directly to Eastern religions. Beat politics was liberal, leaning toward the Left and anti-war, supporting causes like desegregation. They were attracted to jazz music and African-American culture. Some saw the Beat's radical left leanings as an indication of interest in communism, but the only connection between them and the communists was their mutual disregard for capitalism.

The beat generation was the first to attack what they saw as an anachronistic conservative morality in the United States. They advocated for free and open sex and sought Asian philosophy to attain religious enlightenment. They believed that drugs could be a valuable tool to expand spirituality.

The Beats wrote poetry and created art, but the results were second-rate. Freedom was their mantra, freedom from an out-of-date establishment that was repressive. Like postmodernism in the 1970s, the beat generation appealed to academic circles where the new and unusual became faddish. Beat writings and poetry became fashionable. Their style of dress and vocabulary became part of popular culture, and they became the new hipsters.

The New Left
Fast forward to 1964. The writings of the non-conformists Norman Mailer and Susan Sontag exerted significant influence over the American intellectual space. Mailer achieved fame as a novelist based on his psychopathic heroes and emphasis on sexuality. He was the kind of pop icon intellectuals loved to associate with. Sontag became the symbol of radical chic, that person who is ideologically invested in their cause of choice only so far as it advances their social standing. Like Mailer, the emphasis of Sontag's work was on sex and radical politics.

The year 1964 saw the expansion of the cultural revolution. Demonstrations by members of the Free Speech Movement at the University of California Berkeley influenced college campuses nationwide. Early on, the front and center issues were the Vietnam War, housing arrangements for racial minorities, and university investment policies. Those issues quickly grew into a much broader, fully defined political

145

agenda. The main focus was sensibility, a revolution in radical politics, drug abuse, sexual freedom, exotic forms of spirituality, and an anti-bourgeois attitude. In sum, an attack on the intellectual and moral foundations of post-World War II America.

As we discussed previously, the left's ideology subtly and surreptitiously permeated American culture. The universities fell first as anti-capitalist socialist elements began to gain influence by selling their ideology. This effort was guided by postmodernism which took hold in American universities in the late 1970s. Postmodernism attacked the Enlightenment and declared it dead, calling it an anachronism in the postmodern world. Identity politics and social justice efforts were used to tear down American traditions. Today, American higher education institutions do not experience the protests at the center of the 60s movement. Why? Because they have achieved their goal of left ideological dominance. The irony is the same people who cried out for free speech in the 1960s are now willing to censor those who disagree with them.

After the fall of the universities, the mainstream media was next, influenced by journalists who espoused the ideology they learned during their university training. Social media organizations founded by left-leaning individuals emerged as new advocates of the left and censors of the right.

Political Changes
The current takeover of American political ideology and culture would not have been possible without the fracture of

American politics. In the 1990s, the moderates in Congress left the field, and those remaining left and right had a more extreme ideology. Congress became polarized, and the left began to control Congress the way they managed all the other forms of communication. The right reacted against the left's efforts, and America became a tribal state.

Even though the right is under attack from all quarters, it can maintain its strength through numbers, which remain at 30% of the population. Most conservatives cannot be converted into liberals because their morality is innately different and won't change. Conservatives remain a potent force, particularly in government, where conservatives can use their numbers to elect like-minded politicians. Red states elect conservatives to state governments, and the federal government and left-leaning media cannot prevent that from happening.

Attacks on conservatives take two forms: criticism of American traditions and attacks on moral capital, which has been the expression of human social behavior since man came into being.

Traditions
Traditions are beliefs or behaviors with symbolic meaning, expressing a connection with the past and passed down from one generation to the next within a group or society. Examples include holidays or impractical but socio-historically meaningful clothes, like lawyers' wigs or military officers' spurs. The word tradition comes from the

Latin tradere, which means to transmit, to hand over, or to give for safekeeping.

Humans are governed by political traditions, including constitutions and laws, how rules are applied, and how institutions thrive or die. At the same time, counter forces are operating that attack traditions, including industrialization, globalization, socialist ideology, and treatment of specific cultural groups.

Originally, traditions were passed orally, pictorially, and musically before formal writing systems existed. Poetry was used as a device for oral communication. Traditions change slowly, from generation to generation, so individuals living in a society may not be aware of changes to customs that occur during their lifetime.

Traditions are frequently used in political and religious discussions to establish the legitimacy of specific values. In the United States, the Constitution stands as a great example of a tradition that has been sanctified. The Constitution's authors are lauded as great men who helped make the success of our country possible. The document is foundational and perpetually valuable as a guide to preserving and carrying the country forward.

Tradition has long been a political factor because conservative parties possess a stronger affinity for the past than liberal and progressive parties. Conservative parties focus more on principles of natural law, moral order, hierarchy, and social unity. Traditionalists are uncomfortable with the notions of individualism, liberalism, modernity, and social progress. They favor the family, local community, church, and state. The left criticizes that view because traditions are corrupt and should be discarded.

In societies experiencing rapid social change, specific traditions are contested, with competing groups striving to establish the legitimacy of their values. An extreme example of this is the French Revolution, which destroyed ALL the traditions of France. It took that country 80 years to stabilize its government around reestablished traditions.

Moral Capital
Moral capital is the amount of moral connectivity that exists in a society. The term initially appeared in Jonathan Haidt's *The Righteous Mind*. Haidt wrote:

> Moral Capital refers to the degree to which a community possesses interlocking sets of values, virtues, norms, practices, identities, institutions, and technologies that mesh well with evolved psychological mechanisms and thereby enable the community to suppress or regulate selfishness and make cooperation possible.

Social capital measures how the interaction between people can generate efficiency and connectivity. Moral capital goes one level deeper; it describes connectivity with a moral value component. People, who are socially connected, communicate in ways that foster the sharing of opinions and ideas. Morally bound people share a kinship based on common beliefs and satisfaction from belonging and sharing experiences. The psychologist, Abraham Maslow, suggested that humans seek their optimal place based on their motivation on a hierarchy of needs system. Level 3 in his hierarchy, above physiological and safety requirements, is a sense of belonging, a shared set of beliefs, and self-actualization.

There are four types of moral capital: family, local community, moral community, and nationalism or patriotism.

Family
The family is the most fundamental human grouping, as old as man. The moral value of family is the shared life experience and the protection parents provide their children. Men and women lived together and shared the task of raising the children they produced. The relationships within a family have the most robust moral capital because they form the closest personal relationships between and among human beings. Those relationships last a lifetime. When everything crashes in a person's life, the family is a foundation for support. Because the family is the most essential personal connection in human life, it has the most devastating impact when it fails. Broken marriages, domestic violence, and psycho-emotional abuse create real and invisible scars that may extend beyond a lifetime and continue for generations.

Local Community
The local community consists of relationships among friends, neighbors, and co-workers. Individuals often

interact with their local community when not with their families. The local community provides the security of social interaction with others who live and work in the same space. Its moral value is shared experiences, and self-actualization developed through those relationships.

Moral Community
Moral communities are built through participation in any faith, belief, or worship system. The category goes beyond religion because there are moral communities that are not religious. The moral value is socialization, belonging, and feeling part of something important. It exists in organizations with charitable objectives and delivering services to those who need them.

Religions bring together people who share the same belief systems. Their connection follows from community worship service to activities where individuals contribute time to benefit others. Non-religious moral communities are based on shared belief systems. Organizations like the Rotary Club have a set of standards and public service goals required for members. Pursuing those goals builds a more robust connection within the group.

Loyalty to sports teams is another type of moral community. Americans are fanatically involved in sports, and each team in each city has its tribe of followers. Surveys have shown that 70% of millennials are sports fans. A city's fanbase is a moral community because it goes beyond the social community that's part of attending a game. Fans create a family-like atmosphere around their team, worshiping their heroes and carrying the pain of defeat in the hope of future victories.

Sports devotion is an acceptable application of tribalism because it is non-confrontational, and fans understand the point of view of opposition fans. There is an unwritten rule to respect the opponent's fan in the next seat, you want him to lose, but you won't start an argument over his choice of teams.

Patriotism

The broadest of the elements of moral capital is loyalty to the country. Patriotism is the glue that unites a nation. It allows it to endure its most significant challenges and mark its collective triumphs. Patriotism and love of the country connect every ethnic, cultural, social, and political group. Its moral value is a shared culture and a common way of life to protect. Threats to a nation are threats to all its people and galvanize a society into unity of purpose. Moral capital, based on national interests, is the most fragile of the categories because it's impersonal. Patriotism does not come from relationships between individuals but from a perceived connection to fellow citizens based on language, geography, and nationality.

Moral Capital in Operation

Social stability depends on the amount of moral capital in a society. When moral capital is degraded, society becomes less stable. When we consider national unity a fundamental component of moral capital, the challenge of keeping it strong is enormous because patriotism is constantly attacked in a diverse society. When people lose pride in their nation, they discard the values, virtues, and norms that are a part of the national fabric.

Moral capital is not universally good, and there is a risk it might be harnessed for evil purposes, as the Nazis did. The Nazis influenced economic, social, and moral capital as they gained popularity. In Germany, moral capital was enhanced by a nationalistic fervor harvested from the character and traditions of the German people. Unfortunately, the Nazi regime perverted moral capital's patriotic component in ways hidden from the German people until it was too late. The Nazis executed an ideology bent on world conquest and racism. The same ideology used to unite the German nation almost destroyed it.

Another example is the Soviet Union. What started to be a political system intent on implementing Marxian ideology created a despotic dictatorship instead. Moral capital was purposely used, by the Soviet regime, for propaganda purposes and did not reflect the true feelings of the Russian people. When it was needed to hold the government together at the end of the 1980s, the lies showed themselves to be an illusion, and the authoritarian structure collapsed.

The United States has always aspired to be a society built with moral capital. At the time of its founding, its leader's dreams were distilled from its people's moral capital and written into the Constitution.

Religion was a vital component of America's moral capital from the beginning. Many of the first settlers sought to escape religious persecution in Europe and hoped to find religious freedom in America. They came as families, and family was the fundamental unit of colonial settlements. Often the settlers arrived in groups of multiple families because they were members of the same neighborhood or parish in the old country. Colonial towns were small, and neighbors served together as members of town councils.

America remained a country of small towns until well beyond the time of the Constitution. In 1790 there were only five cities with populations greater than 10,000. By 1810, there were ten. By 1840, there were three cities with more than 100,000 inhabitants. Small towns could create a sense of community better than large cities. People knew everyone in their community and shared common values with their friends. They were tribe-like in that family, community, and church were all linked in the same social groups.

During the Revolutionary War, America was divided by loyalty to the Crown and commitment to the colonies. Moral capital, based on patriotism, did not show up until the country became larger and communication was more widespread. America's strength as a nation emerged at the end of World War I when it first stepped onto the world stage. Our engagement in the Great War was late, and we only played a minor role, but America showed it was committed to defending the ideology of the West. America's moral capital peaked when Pearl Harbor was attacked in

1941, as all Americans became brothers and sisters united to destroy those who had attacked us.

Patriotism ebbs and flows depending on unity resulting from threats from the outside. If there is disagreement about the extent of those threats, as in the case of the Viet Nam War, moral capital decreases rather than being enhanced because the country is divided. The 911 attacks created unity across all social groups because the enemy was the enemy of all and the universal threat to the American people.

Maintaining moral capital at a high level is more challenging in the doing rather than wishing it were so. A changing human society often creates disunity because of the political, economic, and social forces placed on it. Decades may pass between periods of unity.

Attack on Moral Capital
Since the 1960s, the attack on moral capital has been relentless. The behaviors that characterized human life for a million years have been discarded as corrupt or, at the very least, obsolete and incompatible with the postmodern world. The driver for this change is the left ideology that demands equality for all social and economic groups.

The American family has changed radically. Divorce rates increased since the last decades of the 20th Century, and more single parents are raising children. Single mothers struggle to juggle work and child care, which often puts them into poverty. About 20% of children lived with a solo parent in 2017. Men and women are getting married later (averaging approximately 28 years old) or cohabitating (8.5 million in 2018) and are not married. Another 35 million live in single-person households, making up 28% of all households. Thirty-two percent of adults over 15 years old have never been married. Marriage has been redefined and no longer refers to a union between a man and a woman. The women's movement has characterized traditional marriage, mainly where the wife does not work, as a disloyal or inappropriate role for a woman. These women are traitors to the cause because they don't seek self-actualization.

Changes in the local community have resulted from changes in the family and the pace of life. Families have less time and money, which directly impacts social engagement. Parents transport kids to their many activities, filling up any spare time. Parents' fear of harm to their children translates into constant supervision. Movement from the city to the suburbs separates people, breaking up old neighborhood relationships. Television and the Internet have become stay-at-home entertainment platforms, substituting for social connections. Social club membership dropped significantly from 1960 to 2000. People entertain in their homes less frequently and visit their neighbor's homes less often as well. This data is documented in Robert Putnam's (1941-) book *Bowling Alone* (2000).

Changes in the social community structure are due to an active campaign by the left. They are primarily due to the social changes described above and the two-decade trend toward isolation caused by social media and smartphones. Once children reach a certain age, they become estranged from their parents through an addiction to electronic devices. Children play games and communicate with friends over social media as a replacement for interaction within the family. If it becomes weaponized, social media can destroy lives. Electronic bullying is pervasive and causes great pain for those under attack. Psychological problems and even suicide are expected outcomes.

Putnam discusses an idea he calls the dark side of social capital. A study of group behavior in the United States shows that fraternity (feeling like someone belongs to a group that shares their interests), equality, and liberty are always forces in tension. As community participation has decreased in the past 40 years, social equality (as measured by tolerance) has increased. Americans are more tolerant than they used to be of those who behave differently than they do. The problem with this change is that individual liberty is threatened by those who force equality on all.

Traditional religion is under constant attack
Moral community involvement has waned in recent decades. Religious participation dropped 10% between 1960 and 2000. Meanwhile, the percentage of people who say they are not religious has quadrupled. The left celebrates this trend as appropriate for the postmodern society because it considers religious people ignorant cult members who cling to out-of-date traditions.

Left ideology does not accept traditional religion as a valid component of American culture because the socialist vision is secular and anti-God. Socialists see the link between

157

religion and tradition as an obstacle to progress because progress requires change. The left's idea of a perfect secular world requires a commitment to equality. The religious tradition includes errors of thought, so the only way to eliminate those errors is to cancel religion. The left sees religion as bigoted and rigid regarding social values. It wishes to impose its view of fairness on all Americans, assuming that right and wrong are absolutes. The truth will be forced on religious people if they do not compromise their beliefs.

The mistake the left makes, as pointed out by Jonathan Haidt, is the compensating value moral capital provides to human society. Religious groups' deep relationships and shared experiences help unite society.

Patriotism Under Attack
As every American knows, Patriotism and pride in our country have diminished. One reason for this change is the federal government's political logjam and the government's inability to meet the public's needs. In the public's view, politicians act in their interests, dictated by lobbyist money, that keeps them in office. Polls provide a gauge of the support the public has for their elected officials. The last time this number was above 50% was 2005, so we are in a 17-year cycle of dissatisfaction with our government.

Loss of respect for government diminishes pride and patriotism. A society is united when most people feel they are moving forward together and the government is responsive to their needs. Ineffective government breaks that link.

Patriotism is under constant attack from the radical left, which believes that America has committed sins in the past and those sins are proof of a corrupt system. Attacking our history also attacks our founding principles, causing people to question the system's validity. Another issue is the loneliness people feel because their national community is declining.

Many Americans feel a sense of unease over rapid changes in our society over the last decades. That unease was a contributor to tribalism. As discussed in Chapter 6, the eroding of traditions is fundamental to the Marxist/Socialist playbook. It specifies that traditions must be attacked and destroyed to change a political system. Americans must oppose these overt attempts to replace our freedoms.

CHAPTER TWELVE

THE FAILURE OF CONSERVATISM

Conservatism clings to what has been established, fearing that, once we begin to question the beliefs that we have inherited, all the values of life will be destroyed. **Morris Raphael Cohen**

Conservatives possess a political morality unsuited for political warfare. They are not as aggressive as liberals and don't want to be. Conservatives only get motivated when political attacks are aimed at the heart of their beliefs, as was the case during the Equal Rights Amendment ratification attempt in 1972. In that situation, conservatives marshaled together a country-wide effort, changed the public's perception of the issue, and won the battle. Lately, they have been active in the effort to overturn Roe v. Wade and resisting attempts by the left to control what students learn in school. The left continues to push its agenda, using its media control for leverage.

A second reason conservatives are not avid about taking on liberals is that they would rather live in peace than try to change the world. Individualism is a conservative trademark; conservatives expect success to result from their efforts without anyone else's help. They reject government action that makes it more difficult for them to achieve success, like higher taxes. Conservatives are groups because they exemplify loyalty and respect authority. Conservatives are comfortable living in a hierarchical society because they believe that is human society's "natural" structure. They have always resisted rapid societal changes when considering those changes risky and unjustified.

Conservatism, as a political idea, originated in the United Kingdom near the end of the Enlightenment period. Its first great ideologue was Edmund Burke, a member of the British Parliament. Burke was a critic of the Enlightenment, concerned that the foundations of society would be lost if society's traditions were discarded. He viewed the French Revolution as a real-world example of that problem. Burke's ideas contributed to the foundation of the Conservative Party in Britain.

The first link between conservativism and politics in the United States was made with the formation of the Republican Party in 1854. Abraham Lincoln believed in the historical importance of the Constitution as an instrument that held the republic together. He would not allow the South to secede and destroy the United States, but he also wanted to stop slavery in the new states. With war looming, Lincoln understood that the North had to win for the country to be united again. After the war, the assassination of Lincoln forced the Republican Party to move forward without him.

It spent ten years managing reconstruction and building a new party platform that would appeal to the American people.

From 1880 to 1950, the Republican Party supported business, except during the early years of the Progressive Era when it fought for an end to worker exploitation and political corruption. Teddy Roosevelt built a solid progressive platform, and for a time, was by the Republican Party carried the progressive banner. Later, during the New Deal Era, Republicans opposed the programs of Franklin Roosevelt because the new welfare state looked too much like socialism.

After World War II ended, conservatives started thinking about their role in American politics. Long criticized for lacking an ideology, they began to look back at American history in search of an identity. Conservative intellectuals did their research and created a conservative coalition through a partnership between traditionalist conservatives, libertarians, and former communists who had abandoned their cause. By the mid-1950s, the American conservative movement had become a vigorous, if heterogenous, party ready to challenge the New Deal legacy. It lacked cohesion and a unified intellectual foundation to validate its positions.

During the 1960s and 1970s, the conservative ideology matured further. A second wave of former communists joined the coalition and came to be called neoconservatives. They were more tolerant of the welfare state than traditional conservatives and more aggressive toward foreign policy.

By 1980, conservatives had built a sound ideological framework, which helped elect Ronald Reagan as the conservative president since Herbert Hoover.

Reagan's victory led to complacency among conservative intellectuals. They became enamored with the political side of conservativism and abandoned the intellectual side. That split caused the Republicans to lose touch with issues that mattered to the American people. The party's relationship with the Moral Majority, a religion-based particular interest group, contributed to its isolation from mainstream cultural currents.

Conservatives After the Cold War
Conservatives rejoiced with the fall of communism and the breakup of the Soviet Union but also realized the ideological dilemma it created for them. Anti-communism was one of the three pillars of the conservative movement, which helped hold it together in the 1950s and beyond. Would the fall of the Soviet Union destroy its delicate mix of ideologies?

Bob Tyrrell (1943-), editor of the American Spectator, published *The Conservative Crack-up* (1992) in response to the confused state of the conservative movement. Tyrrell argued that even though conservatives made headway in electoral politics, they had lost the battle for the American cultural narrative, which was now firmly in the hands of the left. A disillusioned ex-conservative, Michael Lind (1962-), wrote that the conservative intellectual movement had become hopelessly divided between an elite intelligent minority and a vulgar populist mass. The intellectuals were trying to refine the conservative ideology, but that effort was diluted by conservative politicians who only cared about winning elections.

Effect of 21st-Century Politics on Conservative Ideology

21st Century politics have significantly impacted ideological conservatives. As stated, the conservative ideology after 1960 comprised a coalition of traditionalists, libertarians, and anti-communists. In the 1970s, the neoconservative movement divided the existing doctrine by advocating for a more aggressive approach to foreign policy. Then, in the 1980s, another faction appeared the paleoconservatives. The Paleos wanted to purge the neocons out of the conservative movement and return to the old conservative ideology. The neocon faction prevailed but then withered during the George W. Bush Iraq/Afghanistan war years when the American people grew tired of war. That left the traditionalists and the libertarians to try and pick up the pieces.

The Bush, Obama, and Trump administrations each impacted conservative ideology differently. Bush was a neocon, Obama was a progressive, and Trump a non-ideologue. The ideologues had to accept Bush, warts, and all, because he met the minimum requirement for the conservative label. Obama pushed conservatives to the background, and they broke into factions during their time in the wilderness. In the case of Trump, the ideologues had to live with a candidate who was Republican in name only, offended the traditional party types, and wasn't dependent on the financial leverage typically used to control candidate behavior.

Trump's victory was not that surprising to scholars of American politics, especially those who study the right. His win was hardly preordained, but his primary and general election triumphs fit the trajectory of Republican politics in recent decades. From that perspective, both Trump's candidacy and his electoral college success were decades in the making, even if the outcome was anything but certain on Election Day 2016. Trump tried to redefine conservatism by focusing on middle-class working men, who had been disenfranchised by globalism and discarded by the Democratic Party. That group became an enthusiastic base of support for him that remains today. Trump's victory required rethinking Republican politics and its identity in the 21st Century.

Conservative intellectuals have been concerned about party disunity for years. During the 2008 primaries, David Frum (1960-), a Canadian-American political commentator, warned that the founding principles of American conservatism were under attack and the party could fall apart. Republicans increasingly appeared divided, publicly and privately, over the conservative movement and their party's economic, social, and foreign policy agendas. Some party planks conflicted with others. Cutting spending, a core component of the conservative ideology did not sit well with hawks who wanted aggressive engagement in international affairs. Supportable domestic spending has been a nonstarter with the traditionalists, who don't believe in big government.

Disunity was vital in the divisive, crowded Republican primaries of 2008, 2012, and 2016 when the party struggled to find someone capable of winning back their base in the primaries and winning the general election. Even Trump failed to win a majority of voters in early contests. He won the nomination because the votes were split among many candidates. To his followers, ideology was not as important as getting things done.

Conservatism, like any political ideology, is ripe for criticism from the opposition. Extreme right conservatives are particularly vulnerable to disparagement because their ideology is more rigid and farther from the mainstream. Conservatives have never been good at defending their positions because, for the longest time, they had no intellectually derived ideological principles. It's hard to protect oneself and one's ideology without a coherent story behind the arguments. In addition, conservatives think at an intuitive level, not a logical level. Once established, their moral foundations propel gut-level automatic responses to decision-making. The left employs a more analytical strategy for decision-making because they think differently.

General Criticisms of Conservatives
From a general standpoint, criticism of Conservatives has changed over time based on their evolving ideology. For most of American history, opponents ignored conservatives

as unworthy adversaries. Why bother acknowledging an opponent who has no intellectually derived doctrine?

Before 1950, there was no conservative ideology, per se, only a traditional point of view, so criticisms focused on conservatives' resistance to change, support of business, and focus on tradition. Critics have long asserted that conservatives have an inborn inclination to be negative, making them resist change. To the left, conservatives were disconnected from reality because they reacted against change without understanding its value.

Conservatives are criticized for taking opposite positions on the same issue at different times. For example, they oppose foreign intervention during one time period and support it during another. This change in position is proof to critics there is no true conservative ideology. This argument is faulty, though, because it denies the historical foundations of conservatism, which rely on traditions, even when they evolve.

Conservatives receive criticism for opposing a secular philosophy. They tend to be theistic, which refers to a belief in God, rather than deistic, which refers to the belief in natural gods, or agnostic, which refers to questioning whether God exists. They disagree with the liberal opinion that man can achieve perfection independently. Conservatives have remained religious believers, while the left has moved away from religion, claiming they are emancipated from the superstitions and primitive beliefs most religions advocate.

Conservatives adhere to order and the symbols that justify and sustain them. They believe in the continuity of experience, the historical patterns that provide clues to the future. They believe in an orthodoxy of tradition that includes moral order. Conservative morality is a break against anarchy and an anchor that protects society from mob rule. Conservatives distrust unbounded human nature, a concern for the American founders, who sought ways to build a political system that protected the people against too much democracy.

Despite seeming immoral to the left, conservatives understand the necessity of inequality as a byproduct of capitalism. They believe unequal wealth results from the structure of advanced human society and is an essential aspect of the capitalist function-reward principle. In other words, the hardest workers are entitled to the most significant benefit from their labor. Conservatives believe human beings are not guaranteed success in life, nor are all human beings capable of achieving the same level of success, so they resist efforts to go against nature to create an egalitarian society. They cite evidence of socialist and communist failures as proof that human beings cannot achieve utopia.

Conservatives want government power to be limited. A political system must restrict the operation of majority rule so it remains controlled and supports a pluralistic society. Big government is a stepping stone to a planned society, so conservatives are suspicious of welfare state trends because of their inefficiency, corruption, and negative impact on the free market operation.

Conservatives are defenders of private property before they are defenders of capitalism. Private property has been a part of human society for thousands of years, while capitalism is a product of the Enlightenment.

Specific Criticisms of Conservatives

Frederick Hayek, the Austrian economist, criticized the conservatives, in 1960, for having no ideology. He recognized that conservatism was legitimate and necessary in its role to resist political efforts for change when the value of change was unknown. However, without their ideology, conservatives were destined to be dragged along a path, not their choosing. Hayek said of conservatives,

> When I say that the conservative lacks principles, I do not mean to suggest that he lacks moral conviction. The typical conservative is indeed usually a man of very strong moral convictions. What I mean is he has no political principles which enable him to work with people whose moral values differ from his own for a political order in which both can obey their convictions.[45]

---

[45] Hayek, Fredrich, 1960. *Why I am not a Conservative*. In *The Constitution of Liberty*. Chicago, The University of Chicago Press.

After 1960, it took years for the conservative ideology to become established because conservative intellectuals were too fragmented to unite a unified set of ideas to move forward. Conservatism has always been an amalgam, based on intellectual positions linked as cousins, not brothers.

Criticisms from the left vary, depending on which component of the conservative ideology they choose to attack. The "refuse to change" criticism against traditionalists has been constant over the decades. The left's hatred of capitalism has always driven attacks on the libertarian faction. Liberals can't execute their welfare state ambitions without big government, and libertarians oppose it.

The anti-communists, operating within the conservative tent, were criticized for using a different approach. Since liberals were opposed to communist expansionism themselves, they could not blame the anti-communists for sharing the same beliefs. Instead, they let the former communists take criticism from other conservatives. The conservative camp did not fully trust these converts to commit to its ideology. Were they just liberals in disguise?

Tradition and the Rejection of Evolution
The Enlightenment was built on rational thinking; man could use reason to understand the world and use acquired knowledge to make the world a better place. This idea has proven valid a thousand times over through improvements to health, health care, food standards, and exercise promotion. With the theory of evolution, Darwin stunned the

world with ideas about the development of life resulting from adaptations to living on Earth. Conservatives are often criticized for rejecting evolution as the truth. Forty-three percent of Republicans believe the earth's creatures have evolved, while forty-eight percent believe humans have had the same form since they appeared on Earth. Among Democrats and independents, the percentages accepting evolution are in the mid to upper sixties.

Religion is certainly a factor in human views on evolution. Because its concepts differ from Bible teachings, there is a fundamental incompatibility; the more robust the religious beliefs, the more likely the individual will reject the theory of evolution. At every opportunity, the left happily points out that the conservative rejection of evolution means they reject all of science, which is invalid. Many religious conservatives say they can accept science and religion, no matter their views about evolution.

Tension Between the Party and the Ideologues

There has always been tension between the Republican Party people and the conservative ideologues. The party needs to select electable candidates, and this objective conflicts with the ideologue's desire to maintain their principles. This issue is less significant for the left, where politicians are more tightly aligned with ideologues.

Today the left has a free hand to influence the American political debate because their adversary is too distracted or uninterested in battle. The defeat of Trump left the lingering odor of "what will Trump do next" hanging over the

Republican Party. The party doesn't know how to move past Trump because they can't ignore his constituency. It holds the keys to the next election. Attacking Trump endangers any candidate who must rely on his voting bloc. It also diminishes the conservative response to the excesses of the left. The only solution for the party in 2024 is to give the Trump voting block good reasons to switch to another candidate.

The Authoritarian Right

A growing problem in American politics is the authoritarian right, which consists of disaffected workers, radicals, Alt-right, neo-Nazis, and others. These people are pathologically attracted to authoritarian concepts such as power, master race theory, and bigotry against specific groups. They are authoritarian socialists and not conservatives, although many vote Republican. Conservatives favor the individual over the group and are not interested in centralized authoritarian governments. Trump has led these groups on through his carelessness and never denounced them. His relationship with them casts a shadow on Trump's intentions, making him appear complicit.

Conservatism has not maintained its genetic role

As discussed elsewhere in this book, conservatism is a genetically-based adaptation designed to allow man greater flexibility in adapting to heterogeneous environments. The adaptions which generated conservative thinking were supposed to put a brake on the change advocated by liberals and progressives. In the primitive environment, conservatives were equal to liberals because consensus made

173

decisions. Moreover, the conservative skill of managing a food supply was an asset that had to be respected.

After agriculture began, conservatives had positions of power because their political morality was compatible with the authoritarian structure of early governments. They were better able to lead in those political systems because of their focus on loyalty and authority as governing principles. The Enlightenment reshuffled the cards, allowing liberals to advocate for a new government. Liberals and conservatives were now equals and fought for control of American politics until the beginning of the 21st Century.

Today the deck is further stacked against the conservatives. The left's control of the means of education and communication in America allowed them to broadcast their ideology repeatedly. The more it is heard, the more it is believed.

CHAPTER THIRTEEN

WHY MORAL BALANCE MATTERS

The physical world seeks balance to avoid instability. That applies to physics, chemistry, and morality. **Unknown**

As we discussed in chapter two, environmental adaptation was a characteristic that allowed man to survive the challenges of life on this planet and avoid the extinction that doomed his fellow hominids. His omnivore diet made him a flexible eater, improving the chances of finding food in any climate. His bipedalism permitted a man to run swiftly when hunting. His opposed thumb facilitated the use of tools. Most importantly, his brain developed the critical functions of intelligence, including the socialization skills needed to work with other humans.

We discussed polymorphism, the biological adaptation where genes are expressed in multiple forms. Evolutionary pressure caused a polymorphism of adaptive behaviors to develop in man so he could be more flexible in adapting to heterogeneous environments. The resulting adaptation produced a spectrum of behaviors ranging from liberal (hunters) to conservative (managers). Liberals sought what was new and were drawn to change, while conservatives were more comfortable with the status quo and didn't like change. In a small group organization, liberals and conservatives checked each other. Their decisions were made by a group that involved input from both sides to create consensus and prevent errors in judgment.

Change is constant in society through generational or change within a single generation. The world is dynamic, so conservatives have always had to accept change as a part of life. Their degree of acceptance of change depends on the rate of change. Conservatives use tradition as evidence for moderating the rate of change in society.

Political Morality
Political morality, in a society, is the set of behaviors that society will allow without punishment, expressed through the passage of laws and the adoption of customs. To function as a member of a society, people must set aside their morality when it conflicts with the morality of society. As Freud pointed out in his book *Civilization and Its Discontents,* the individual must be able to suppress natural urges that were normal in a tribal setting.

After the beginning of agriculture, governmental power was controlled by the wealthy, those able to exploit their intellect or those who could lead an army. Most often, that power was in the hands of conservatives, who placed value on loyalty and authority. Liberals had no work in those governments because the public had no rights or welfare systems.

Occasionally people could influence the government by applying leverage based on their ability to organize in numbers. In Ancient Rome, after the republic was created, the plebeians went on strike demanding representation in government. As a result of this demand, the Tribunate magistracy was designed to satisfy their need. In history, examples like this were often the exception rather than the rule.

The Enlightenment began as an awakening or intellectual rebirth of classical thinking and ideas. The centerpiece of that remarkable era was the recognition of individual rights. Citizens began to reject the divine right of kings and the church to make laws without their approval. Monarchies were exposed as illegitimate seats of power that operated for the crown's benefit, not the people.

The American Revolution, an experiment in Enlightenment thinking, led toward the implementation of political systems with citizens' rights. Those rights included laws protecting the people from the power of government. For the first time since the advent of agriculture, liberals could participate in government and employ their natural beliefs to better society. Liberals began to fight for welfare programs to be enacted, asserting that it was the government's responsibility to protect its people.

By the end of the Enlightenment period, capitalism had become the driver for a new age of technology and industrialization. This expansion of business, opportunities for entrepreneurship, and improvements in standards of living were significant accomplishments of Western economies. However, that progress came at a price because the masters of the industrial revolution ignored workers' rights. As industrialization expanded, workers became the slaves of industry.

The Progressive Movement became prominent after 1880, attacking worker exploitation and political corruption. That force led to a social justice philosophy in the United States. Reformers fought for workers to receive management concessions, which shortened their work day and made jobs less hazardous. The movement drove the effort to reduce city corruption, forcing the states to set up autonomous city governments. After decades of action, the Women's Movement finally obtained the right to vote in 1920. In the beginning, the Progressive Movement was driven by conservatives, but it migrated to the Democrats following the presidency of Theodore Roosevelt. After Roosevelt, no conservative voice represented the progressive, so President Wilson became the progressive's new voice.

Social justice expanded during the Depression when the federal welfare state system was introduced. Congress passed the Social Security Act of 1935, which provided a retirement pension for American workers. Early in his presidency, Franklin Roosevelt partnered with the progressives, but later he abandoned them because he needed the support of the corporations to implement his programs. After World War II, the Progressive Movement disappeared because its links to communists had tainted it. New Deal Liberalism continued into the 1950s, opposing the capitalist Republicans. The two parties were equally influential during this period and traded federal government control.

The prosperity of the 1950s evaporated in the 1960s when the counterculture movement called into question the traditional view of American life. During that period, the Vietnam War was criticized, and the Civil Rights movement pressured the federal government to pass laws extending equality to African-Americans. Protests and riots were included in the attacks on the government and reached a climax at the Democratic political convention in Chicago in 1968.

A New Left ideology emerged from the counterculture movement as progressives returned. They moved strongly into academia and gained influence there. In the decades after the 1970s, liberals and progressives increased their power, first in the traditional media and then, after 2000, in the new media. These "new" progressives' primary focus was identity politics, derived initially from socialist theory. Identity politics grew from genuine concern over the rights of certain minority groups to a left-driven dogmatic view of the world that rejects any opposing idea.

Since the Reagan years, the right has been on the defensive, struggling to define its ideology in a way that will win votes from the American people. The conservative ideology is fragmented, an obstacle in its quest to win the presidency. Conservatives have forfeited their chance to blunt the left's recent culture war attacks because they are unwilling to show flexibility.

The left is much more unified than the right, allowing them to apply their ideology's full force through their media loudspeaker. Recently emboldened by the Biden election, the left is utilizing these assets to take over American society and put it on a path to implementing a socialist government.

Balance in the Physical World
Science shows us balance in the physical world is fundamental, and forces always move toward equilibrium. When a chemical reaction reaches equilibrium, the result is a steady state. A fire burns out when all the fuel (e.g., wood) is consumed. The fire has reached equilibrium. The same principle applies to the transfer of heat. If a warm object, like a cup of coffee, is placed on a table, it will lose heat in the air until it cools to the temperature of its surroundings. When the temperature of the coffee reaches the temperature of the air, there is equilibrium.

Balance in Politics
In politics, power ebbs and flows between the parties. Human nature dictates those in power will act to retain and expand their power. In pursuing that objective, they adopt more extreme ideas because those with the most robust ideological views influence them. As the party in power moves further toward the extreme, they are opposed by those with more moderate points of view. Those in the middle, who are not ideologues, join the opposition if they feel uncomfortable with the direction being taken. Eventually,

the powerful are defeated, and the political system returns to equilibrium.

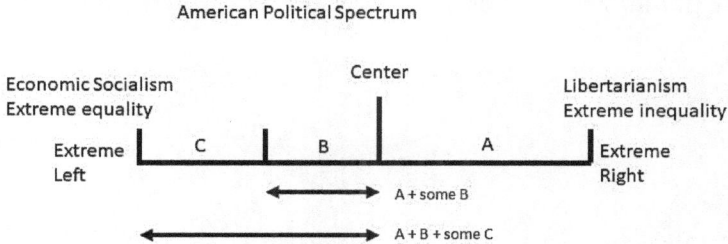

American Political Spectrum

Economic Socialism
Extreme equality

Center

Libertarianism
Extreme inequality

Extreme
Left

C

B

A

Extreme
Right

A + some B

A + B + some C

The chart above shows the forces that balance the American political system. On the right is unfettered capitalism, which would produce extreme inequality if implemented. Libertarians believe in minimal government. In their world, the government should provide no programs for the disadvantaged. At the opposite end of the political spectrum is economic socialism, the utopian world of socialist equality. Since the Biden election in 2020, progressives have been trying to move America further to the left. The two-way arrows show how the amount of resistance depends on the distance from the center. If Democrats move left from the center to the first vertical bar, there will be resistance from the right and some centrist voters on the left (A + some B). If they move to the second vertical bar, the opposition will increase to include many more on the left who will question the extreme (A + B + some C). Most Americans favor capitalism and don't want it replaced by socialism. Those who prefer socialism include younger voters who don't understand what socialism is.

Over time, the back-and-forth swings in political control have been a reality since the United States was established.

181

One party gains popularity and is supported by the public. Later, that party becomes more extreme, governs poorly, or the public wants change, so they are removed from office.

Conservative vs. Liberal Control of Congress

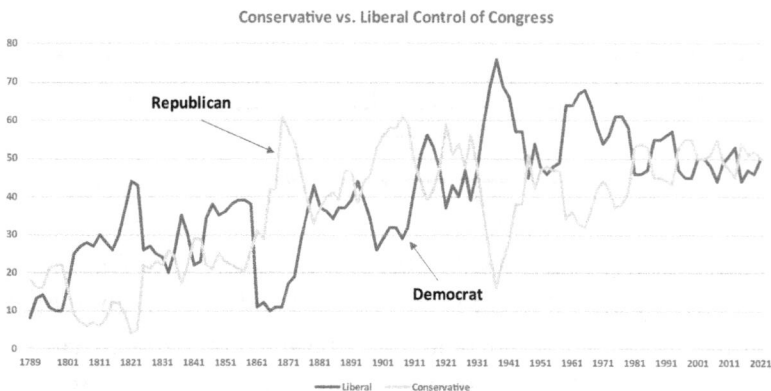

The chart above shows the party control of the Senate since the United States government was established. Liberals are marked in black, and conservatives are marked in gray. The numbers on the vertical axis show the number of senators for each party during that year. Two extreme cases occurred: in 1861, the start of the Civil War when the Southern states seceded and left the Republicans with a supermajority, and during the Great Depression, when Republicans were blamed for the stock market crash, and the Roosevelt administration gained total control of the government.

This rebalancing mechanism helps prevent one party from moving too far from the center, operating in the same way as the left-right balancing adaptation in operation during the time of primitive man.

Balance in Power Institutions

A government with unbalanced power is essential as a source of influence over American society, but that is only one power source. Others include the educational system, the communication systems (media), and traditions representing behavioral norms produced from historical experience. In the United States, all these institutions have tilted left, except for traditions, which have always been part of the conservative ideology. That leftward tilt is constant no matter which side holds the power in government. Today, left-leaning institutions have virtually eliminated counterforces that could mitigate their impact.

Most of the faculty positions in universities are now held by liberals and progressives, while conservatives hold fewer and fewer. Academia has evolved throughout history based on expanding knowledge and debate outside politics. In recent decades, universities have discarded foundational concepts favoring dogmatic political positions.

In the 1980s, postmodernism began to infect and take over the humanities. By the 1990s, it was firmly established as the default ideology for the humanities and some of the social sciences. The essence of this ideology was the negation of truth and the rejection of the Enlightenment as a legitimate guide for human society. Postmodernism questions the validity of truth, asserting that truth was a creation of power groups intent on exploiting minority groups.

Anything important in academia eventually becomes essential in American society, so Academia's politicization and move to the left bring their bias directly to the public. The left uses its academic mouthpiece to influence other communication platforms, including traditional and social media.

Balance Among the People
The American people retain genetic differences despite changes in social, cultural, and political. The human moral-political spectrum evolved a million years ago and still operates today.

Unfortunately, in these tribal times, the ability of the right and left to reach a consensus based on discussion and negotiation is impossible. Extreme positions advanced loudly on both sides, drown out balanced positions, so Americans are burdened with conflict. This unrealistic representation of the world psychologically damages the human perception of what living in a society should be like. Tribalism has made people afraid to discuss politics, even with family members.

A Study published in 2018 defined the American political spectrum in detail, showing there are factions within each party in addition to independent groups. The study identified seven groups. The farthest left is the activist progressives, who comprise 8% of the population and are most aggressive about achieving socialist objectives. Next, moving to the right, are traditional liberals, who comprise 11% of the population. That group reflects a baby boomer philosophy of government, supporting social justice, but not as enthusiastically as the progressives do. The third group is the passive liberals, making up 15% of the population. These individuals have a modern view of social issues but are not politically engaged. Two-thirds of this group do not have a college degree. Group four is labeled politically disengaged. They represent an incredible 26% of the population. These people are lower income and are not engaged in politics. They are pessimistic about a solution to tribalism in America. Group five comprises the moderates, who account for 15% of the population. They despise ideologies, and 89% feel political correctness has gone too far. Group six is made up of traditional conservatives, and they represent 19% of the population. They think America is under attack by liberals, although they are open to bipartisanship. The final group comprises devoted conservatives, who comprise 6% of the population. This group is ideologically driven, like the progressives at the other end of the spectrum. They believe in America's traditions and are less likely to compromise than traditional conservatives. Combining the groups by party reveals that 34% are Democrats, 25% are Republicans, 15% are moderates, and 26% are not engaged in politics.

These groups and their characteristics show how political morality is spread across the American population. The features of these groups endure no matter what the politics of the moment may be. No force, idea, or opinion will change the genetic distribution of these groups. Although there are exceptions, liberals can't become conservatives, and conservatives can't become liberals.

Why balance matters

Balance of power and opinion is essential for a healthy human society. As we discussed, polymorphism created a political morality to make man more adaptable. Society becomes unstable when forces in society upset the balance between left and right. Moral balance must function as a brake against irrational action. Without that brake, society will degrade.

Political Failure Without Balance

As much as liberals dislike conservatives, it's a mistake to discount the importance of opposing views on their extreme ideas. Moderate Democrats could bring more sensible ideas to the table, but they remain silent, cowed by the aggression of the progressives as they work to put their ideology into practice. How is that implementation going? Let's look at the example of San Francisco to see the impact of the single-party left rule.

Zach Colieus is the managing partner at Colieus Capital, which invests in startup businesses. On May 5th, 2023,[46] Zach published an impassioned plea on Twitter calling for change to the governmental structure of San Francisco. Zach considers the current government dangerous because it operates without opposition to its radical progressive ideas. Single-party control means no brake on extreme positions. By the way, Zach is a progressive.

The city is run by a board of supervisors and independent committees of appointed cronies who run each department.

---

[46] Colieus, Zach. *San Francisco*. Twitter May 5th 2023.

The mayor cannot be held accountable because the office has no power. Lack of accountability has led to out-of-control spending and focus on ideological success rather than good government. Corruption and ineptitude are endemic.

San Francisco changed its law enforcement and policing policies to implement a progressive ideology. The city stopped enforcing minor crimes and decriminalized shoplifting. The effect of that change was to increase property crimes and expand criminality. Now gangs routinely break into stores and rob them, resulting in enormous property loss.

The city also decided to stop enforcing drug laws, which made it a magnet for addicts and criminals that serve the drug trade. Without law enforcement, there is no risk of arrest. Drug addicts live on the street and take whatever they need from stores. They mix with people experiencing homelessness and occupy sections of the city center. There is no system for placing these people elsewhere because San Francisco has an inadequate housing supply. It is the 3rd most expansive city to live in the United States, and its real estate prices have been driven higher by the demand for technology worker housing. Living space is unavailable to the middle class, pushing more people onto the street or driving them out of the city.

Tourists have stopped coming to the city, offices are empty, and retail stores are closing because of inventory loss. Those businesses that can leave are doing so. Some have said San Francisco is entering a doom loop, a feedback loop of adverse events that reinforce each other and cause a downward spiral.

Similar scenarios are being played out in Detroit, Philadelphia, Chicago, New York, Seattle, and Portland, where the rule of law is being discarded. Decriminalization, light or no sentences for repeat offenders, slashing police budgets, and attacking law enforcement are popular initiatives.

Like the old urban patriarchs, these cities have strong unions, particularly teachers' unions. Public schools are failing, and there are no alternatives because the unions are protected. That protection allowed them to exert power over the school systems during COVID, blocking the education of millions of students. These cities are also "sanctuaries," with programs to protect illegal immigrants from the law. That focus requires them to redirect capital typically earmarked for their permanent citizens. Lately, they have been trying to ship their illegal aliens elsewhere because they can't accommodate them. Unlimited immigration is fine as long as it doesn't involve my city.

The same criticism can be lobbed at right-only governance. The Red States have recently been passing laws that reflect their ideology. For example, some red states have banned all abortions from conception, no matter the mother's circumstances. That demonstrates the expression of a rigid conservative ideology. Like the blue states, red states often place ideology above the best interests of all their constituents in favor of extreme ideologues. Red state efforts are concentrated in the cultural space, not the economic space because red states have no interest in changing the current system of government.

This trend toward ideological state governance is a new layer of tribalism. Each side, liberal and conservative, strongly opposes the opposition viewpoint. That behavior is destructive because it destroys any hope for unity. The left believes it embraces the proper moral narrative for America, and the Right is ignorant and wrong. The left uses its control of the media to drive that point home.

CHAPTER FOURTEEN

CAN THE AMERICAN EXPERIMENT SURVIVE?

What was the American experiment?
Americans created the first new Western nation in 1000 years, without the cultural baggage carried by Europe after the fall of Rome. Europe persevered by building political systems out of the ashes of the Roman Empire and forging its way through the dark ages to rediscover the value of classical thought. The advent of science and Enlightenment thinking reinvigorated the concept of the individual as central to human society and paved the way for establishing human rights.

Europe's baggage was its commitment to authoritarian power and its alliance with the Catholic Church, which produced centuries of wars, undertaken to expand the power of competing monarchies. Europe's institutions dictated a pitiful existence for private citizens, who had no rights and little opportunity to make their way. Their social class system was rigid and upward mobility was blocked by the tradition of autocratic power.

The United States was the first great Enlightenment political project, a nation created from the ground up with citizen rights built into its political system. Americans harbored beliefs infused with core Enlightenment ideas: innovation, the desire to control one's life, freedom of religion, equal rights for all, and a say in government action. When those beliefs were subverted by the British Crown, the American people chose revolution as the best path to freedom.

The first settlers in North America were rugged idealistic people chasing a dream. Many were naïve about the hardships they would encounter but willing to take a chance on freedom. These new Americans had various reasons for crossing the ocean: escape from poverty and poor economic conditions, freedom from religious persecution, an opportunity to own property, and a desire to build a better life. The early settlement years after 1607 saw thousands die from disease and starvation while farmers used trial and error to find crops that would grow on American soil. In the north, rocky New England would not support agriculture. In the deep South, it was so hot that temperate climate crops would not grow. Economic progress was slow, and it took time for colonies to stabilize. In 1650, only 50,000 people were living in 13 colonies. By 1700, the population had grown to 250,000 as a result of immigration and native growth in the population. During the first century of the American colonies, 200,000 immigrants arrived in America. One-third were free; the others were enslaved people, convicts, or indentured servants.

Sponsors for the original settlements were corporations contracted by the king, who planned to use colonists as laborers to work corporate-owned farms. That model broke down quickly when colonists demanded their land. The landmass of America was so vast there was no advantage to working for a corporation when a person could find available land and set up his farm. To reverse chronic labor shortages, a system of granting free land to individuals was introduced in Virginia in 1619.

During America's first century, most farms in the colonies were owned by single families growing their food for subsistence. Later, as surpluses became more common, crops were sold for profit. An entrepreneurial spirit evolved as each farm was turned into a small business. Owning land became a measure of success and fostered independence. In New England, where farming was impossible, the focus was on business. There, manufacturing and trade became the economic drivers. Lumber was plentiful, and the sea offered an abundance of fish to take to market. Whale oil was needed to light the lamps in colonial homes.

The government was essentially non-existent during the first half of the colonial period. There was no federal government because the crown controlled the colonies. Most colonies had rudimentary legislative bodies akin to the British model: an upper house (Senate) of experienced leaders, a citizen-elected assembly, and a governor. Colonial courts were simplified versions of the British legal system, which relied on precedent rather than statute. The colonial courts had no professionals (lawyers or judges) because there were none available, so a "judge" was appointed among citizens to render decisions. Juries were typically not used because too few citizens were available to serve on them.

The American character, which developed during the first century of the colonial period, matured during the second. That character contained five elements: practicality, independence, understanding the use of violence, privacy, and acquisitiveness. Americans learned to be practical because there was no goods-based economy, and almost all settlements were rural. Each family unit grew its food, made its clothes, and provided protection for itself. Independence was a requirement based on the way life had to be lived. Those who could not fend for themselves had to wait for the establishment of urban environments before settling. People were always drawn to the wilderness, even after cities and towns were established. That drive pushed American expansion westward.

Americans were violent out of necessity. With no government and no police force, life was essentially Darwinian. Weapons were essential to prevent violence against one's family and property and hunt for food. Americans valued privacy, and their property was considered inviolate, not to be trespassed upon or used without permission of the owner. Guns in the home discouraged trespassers.

The fifth characteristic of the American colonist was acquisitiveness, or the desire to accumulate money and possessions. America had no barrier to accumulating wealth and property, so a man could work hard and be rewarded. Everyone was equal under the law, so accumulating wealth was evidence of a rising position in the community and served as a benchmark for social and economic standing.

Characteristics that made Americans different resulted from their unique environment, which drove their perception of the role of government. Government should only perform functions necessary to carry out its role in society: administer the legal system and pass laws designed to protect citizens' rights. Government must never infringe on the rights and liberty of the people.

The Constitutional Convention did not create a Bill of Rights because there was disagreement among the delegates on whether one was needed. By September of 1787, after months of debate over the Constitution, during a hot Philadelphia summer, even the pro-Bill of Rights convention delegates didn't have the energy to create one. After the convention, there was significant pushback from some states who refused to ratify the Constitution without a Bill of Rights. James Madison volunteered to draft the bill, fearing the passage of the Constitution was now in jeopardy. Madison used several sources for his draft, including The English Bill of Rights and The Virginia Declaration of Rights.

Madison put together a list of twelve amendments for consideration. Ten were selected and became the Bill of Rights. Several specifically address the freedoms Americans believed were fundamental. Amendment One, Freedom of speech, was used in the Virginia Declaration of Rights and the English Constitution. It described freedom of speech, religion, and assembly. A free press was also guaranteed. Free speech originated with the Greeks and became prominent in British political thinking after the Glorious Revolution in 1688.

Amendment 2, the right to bear arms, had specific applicability in America because of the existence of separate states. The amendment gave each state the right to keep its militia to defend itself. The Virginia Declaration of Rights specified militias as a safe body of citizens instead of a potentially dangerous national standing army. The English Constitution permitted the carrying of firearms by the public as a guarantee for their safety.

Amendment 3, no quartering soldiers in someone's house without permission, addressed the American belief in private property and the individual's control over his property. The British army violated this freedom before the revolution when British soldiers were housed in Massachusetts homes. Its precedent is the British Constitution.

Amendment 4 prohibited unreasonable searches without a warrant. Like the others, amendment 4 protects the rights of an individual against unfair use of governmental power. A government-controlled judiciary can be corrupted if not held in check by rules that protect the privacy of citizens and their possessions. This amendment was taken from the Virginia Declaration of Rights.

Amendment 5 requires indictment by a grand jury and bars a defendant from testifying against himself.

Amendment 6 requires a speedy trial and the ability of the accused to confront his accusers. The accused is entitled to representation and to call witnesses on his behalf. The words for this amendment were taken from the Virginia Declaration of Rights.

The Bill of Rights was the legal expression of three fundamental characteristics that influenced the foundation of the American political system as a new order. The first of these characteristics was the traditions practiced by the people who settled in America. Those traditions included family, community, and religion. The second characteristic was the people's view of the vast wilderness that made up America and the available land to purchase. Unlimited land meant an unlimited opportunity for man to prosper. Through hard work, Americans could build a new life for themselves. The third characteristic was Enlightenment philosophy. Because America had no pre-Enlightenment baggage to throw off, it could freely apply Enlightenment concepts to the political structure of the new nation. Prominent among these concepts was the value of the individual as the focus of government, people's right to determine their destiny, and limits placed on government power.

The American Experiment Under Attack
America's fundamental beliefs, discussed above, and part of American society since it began, have been under constant attack in the 21st Century. Progressives on the left seek to

break down America's traditions by labeling them obsolete or corrupt. That socialist game plan is not hidden and has been made public for all to see. Anyone on the left, who talks about equality, is using a code word for socialism. True equality requires an authoritarian government to enforce it. The left understands their goal of equality cannot be achieved without tearing down the capitalist democracy we have today. As a reminder of their strategy, consider the socialist playbook discussed previously in Chapter 7. Reread these paragraphs and relate them to the stories you see on the news daily.

Demoralization
A demoralization strategy unfolds when curricula are controlled by leftist ideologues whose goal is to indoctrinate students with a set of values and beliefs foreign to the American tradition. That effort has accelerated over the last ten years with an emphasis on Critical Race Theory and anti-white demagoguery. In the past few years, the federal government and school boards have begun to assert that they, not parents, will determine how children should be educated. That overreach has caused a significant backlash among parents. American traditions are continually assaulted outside the classroom and in the public space. Statues are torn down, religious references ridiculed, and the Constitution attacked.

Demoralization makes people believe the way of life they are used to is ending, precisely what the socialists hope will happen. We hear over and over again how our ancestors exploited and abused the people of their time. Those most susceptible to this propaganda, among us, become anxious and feel guilty for sins that are not their own.

Destabilization

Destabilization is a rapid decline in the structure of a society — degrading law and order, the economy, and the political system. Following the murder of George Floyd, a national effort to defund police departments commenced. Rather than fix the real problems, activists attacked the concept of law enforcement, contending that implementing their ideology was more important than the rule of law. The left has used the criminal justice system's unfair treatment of African-Americans (also affecting poor whites) to indict the whole system. Now criminals are being released from jail en masse, and prosecutions for some crimes have been eliminated. The result? Rampant corruption in large cities, where organized gangs walk into businesses and steal merchandise without the fear of arrest.

The American economy has been destabilized over the issue of climate change. Efforts on the part of the left to accelerate the move to a non-carbon-based energy model have turned the oil companies into pariahs and blocked new drilling and pipeline installation efforts. The current high price of gasoline validated the folly of this tactic. If the United States had retained its position as a net oil exporter, we wouldn't be experiencing the current shortage. The "climate emergency" is false and driven by ideology and those who profit from climate business. There is nothing wrong with sustainability, but it must be implemented at a pace that makes economic sense.

Crisis

Crisis is the third stage of a revolution, and the COVID pandemic provided a convenient opportunity for the left to employ its strategy. COVID was an excuse to impose government-mandated controls over the American population. These controls made sense when little was known about the disease, and there was no treatment, but lockdowns continued well past the time they were effective. As more became known about fighting the disease, governmental bodies should have scaled back these controls, but they did not. Looking back, we see that masks serve no purpose, and lockdowns cause more harm than good. The impact on families forced to stay home was severe. Children were subjected to poorly delivered learning programs or deprived of education altogether. Parents could not work because they couldn't arrange affordable childcare. Depression increased across America, exacerbating drug abuse, mental health problems, and suicide. The American economy was disrupted. Many businesses were closed because of low demand for their products, but more importantly, people lost their jobs and had no income.

The pandemic caused a political divide among the states, with red states choosing to be less restrictive than blue states. It is difficult to understand why blue states did not consider the collateral damage to their constituents. The exercise of governmental control was their primary objective.

Normalization

In the left's mind, the new normal should include reforming the American political system and social structure into a form that replaces the country's founding principles. The new system would be based on the goal of equality as a replacement for economic opportunity.

Some on the left say, "We don't want Marxian socialism; we want democratic socialism," as if there is a difference. In a Marxian society, government controls the means of production. The left imagines a democratic society where people elect socialists, and those individuals exercise control over government action. That government would seek equality through the distribution of wealth across our community. Replacing corporate and capital power with an egalitarian system would not bring equality because no one could guarantee that those in power would rule fairly. The most likely outcome would be the concentration of power in the hands of a few, who would put their welfare above that of the public.

The Drift Left of the Democratic Party

The Democratic Party and President Biden made a devil's bargain with radical left-wing progressives in 2020. Most Americans assumed Biden would be the same person they observed for decades as a Senator; he was moderate and open to ideas from both sides. During the campaign, Biden said he would unite America, but that was a lie. Most people thought Democrats would gauge the public's mood and act accordingly; they would want to prove Trump's incompetence by showcasing their competence. Instead, Biden assumed the role of tribal leader of his most radical constituents. His agenda has included enlarging the welfare state, moving it toward socialism, and adopting more extreme cultural positions.

The Socialist Party is currently active in California. In 2010, California passed a bill that changed the primary election format to what is referred to as a "jungle" primary. The top two vote-getters in each direct move on to the general election regardless of their party affiliation. So, for example, two Democrats may oppose each other for the same office. For several years, the Republican Party experienced a decrease in popularity and currently holds only a tiny percentage of state-wide offices. In 2022, 20% of the state elections had no Republican candidate. That vacuum opened the door for socialists to get into the game. There is currently one socialist serving as a state assemblyman, and several socialists have been elected to local office, including the mayor of Oakland. Socialists are busy building coalitions that will help them win more elections. How far will they be able to extend their influence?

Moral Balance

The thesis of this book is that moral balance is necessary for our republic to function and why an unbalanced political system places America at risk. Political morality must be reflected in a society's institutions. Higher education should return to the principles fundamental to its creation, the open debate of ideas. Mainstream media should report the news fairly and not favor one political ideology. Social media should be barred from censoring material from any particular political group. Politics should not be a part of institutions that educate and inform the public.

Man has experienced three significant social milestones since he came into existence. The first was the advent of agriculture. Agriculture made dense populations possible and led to the development of towns and cities. Those societies evolved a political morality out of necessity, detached from the individual or individual's social group. To be a part of a society, one has to conform to the morality (laws) created by the state. From the beginning of agriculture to the Enlightenment, conservatives ruled. Why? Because the commoner had no rights and societies were based on authority and loyalty, hallmark moral positions of conservatives.

The second critical period was the Enlightenment, when people demanded that authoritarian governments be discarded because they didn't recognize the rights of individuals. Everyone must have the right to control their own life and live as they choose, so accomplishing that goal depends on their ability to influence the government. The Enlightenment unleashed an era of free-thinking, leading to the development of science, democratic political systems, and capitalism. It awoke sleeping liberals, who could now begin their fight for justice and equality. Liberal thinkers created economic and moral socialism as political ideologies to compete with democracy. After the Industrial Revolution began to take its toll on Western society, liberals increased their power by organizing and attacking the rampant inequality and corruption in American society.

Today, America is in its third stage of societal evolution, characterized by the left's dominance. This change began, in the 1960s, when the counterculture movement began to attack America's traditions. During the latter stages of the 20th Century, private institutions moved left. Academia was the first victim when graduates of the counterculture movement became professors at universities. Mainstream media followed because of the influence of academia on the profession of journalism. The advent of the internet and cell phones fostered the explosive growth of social media, and it became a left-leaning forum representing west coast progressive ideology.

During the early decades of the 21st Century, America separated itself into tribes as the political center fell away and only extreme points of view remained. The left is using ideology to attack American traditions, claiming that American history is corrupt and represents only the exercise of power by white men. This attack seeks to tear down the traditional family, cancel religion, and discard patriotism as misguided. The left's "woke" point of view requires that everything possible should be done to reshape America into an egalitarian society.

COVID

The COVID pandemic had a traumatic impact on American society for several reasons. First, there was the lethal character of the disease and no way to fight it. Secondly, the government's response, both at the national and state level, profoundly impacted the American way of life. The federal government implemented emergency procedures to try and limit the spread of disease and avoid overtaxing the healthcare system. In 2021, the government began to deviate from its traditional approach of offering non-political public health advice when information about the disease and its treatment was restricted to the left's dogmatic political view. For example, drugs that appeared effective in treating the disease were banned. Public health policies, such as lockdowns and mask-wearing, instituted at the pandemic's beginning, remained in place even when evidence to the contrary began to appear.

Sensing this as a political canard, red states began to move in a different direction. They opened up their economies faster and were less restrictive than blue states. The federal government and blue states attacked the red state approach and accused them of killing people. Undaunted, red states kept to their plan and were able to recover more quickly.

The COVID experience was unnerving because it unleashed unprecedented government meddling in the lives of Americans. The government health agencies (NIH, CDC) were politicized for the first time. Secondly, the federal government-imposed restrictions universally damaged the lives of Americans. Those restrictions were kept in place despite evidence showing the damage was occurring. Thirdly, the federal government encouraged the media to spread lies about the pandemic and suppress information contrary to the government's position. This behavior severely damaged the reputation of the NIH and CDC. More importantly, there has been no retrospective acknowledgment that mistakes were made or that the pandemic should have been handled differently.

Red state blue state divide.

The year 2023 brings another year of American tribalism and further strengthens the divide by partitioning the states. Red and blue states have begun implementing the ideology of their dominant party. A recent Pew study split the political pie into 17 blue states, 22 red states, and 11 purple (could go either way) states. Red states emphasize law and order, fight to pass laws pertaining to cultural issues that match their ideology, keep current voting laws, and try to be fiscally responsible. Blue states mostly oppose law-and-order policies, so they relax prosecution for certain crimes. They continue to spend enormous amounts of money building government programs and raising taxes in their states, passing laws consistent with their ideology, and weakening perceived restrictions to voting laws.

At a Political Crossroads

The American experiment is at a crossroads, and it's unclear what the future looks like for our society and its political system. As we try to navigate the third decade of the 21st Century, there is rough water ahead. Trump's defeat was a setback for the Republican Party, torn by division into opposing factions and had no rudder as of mid-2023. Trump left significant wreckage behind him, but his influence remains significant. Half the Republicans supported him because he was a disrupter and represented those without an advocate. Many believe Trump is the only one who can represent their interests. Polite conservatives despise his vulgarity and hope never to see him again. To them, accomplishments have no value without decorum. The Democratic Party has launched many lawsuits and criminal indictments against Trump, hoping to derail his 2024 candidacy. The only thing gained so far by this activity is the incitement of the left who hate Trump. Republicans believe these proceedings are illegal or not based on evidence. Trump's poll number grows with each new accusation.

AS of mid-2023, the Republican Party finds itself in a box regarding a candidate for the 2024 election. Party leaders would like to move on from Trump to a more mainstream candidate, but Trump voters are sticking with their man. Those voters have a suicide pact with their leader and will vote for him even if, in doing so, they reelect Joe Biden or another Democrat.

Catastrophe without Balance

What is the impact on a society when external and internal pressures degrade the ability of that society to function? Collapse or change?

Human history includes many cases where societies collapsed. The fall of the Roman Empire is the most common example, although the word collapse is misleading. The Roman Empire evolved with the socio-political landscape in Europe and the Middle East and did not end at a fixed point. As Rome faded away, other institutions replaced it. The Eastern Roman Empire survived until 1453 CE, when the Ottoman Turks took control of the Byzantine Empire.

There have been actual collapses in history, including the Mesopotamian culture, which collapsed several times. Other notable examples include the Teotihuacan culture of Mexico and the Han Dynasty in China. External factors can undoubtedly cause the collapse of society. When a nation loses a war, as Germany did in World War II, its government collapses. The German society and culture survived their defeat, rebuilt their country, and implemented a new political system.

What about internal factors?

A major internal factor contributing to the disruption of a political society is division within the ruling elite. This group typically includes intellectuals, the wealthy, elected officials, religious leaders, and those who enjoy great popularity. When groups with the most significant influence are united and cohesive, they strengthen and support each other. A coherent structure moves forward because power is evenly distributed. However, group cohesion is disrupted when one group obtains complete control of the levers of power. A narrowing of vision results because the policies of the controlling power are based on their viewpoint, ignoring the views of others. As factions become more tribal, each claims moral preeminence over the other. Struggles between them become more rancorous, even violent.

The energy that had once gone into the maintenance and advancement of the political system is now consumed by battles among adversaries. Critical decisions that benefit the whole society are ignored, and confidence in the effectiveness of the ruling elite begins to crumble. Important symbols and doctrines used to build the political system are now disputed.

The people, observing this split among the ruling class, gravitate to one or the other, whichever matches their political morality. This migration seems to prop up the existing order, but it's a canard. The new power brokers must act only on those ideas that got them into power, nothing else, so they can't expand their base to stabilize their power. Governing to enjoy the approval of favored elites generates obedience from their tribe and ridicule from the other. Failure to govern turns compliance into disobedience from both sides.

The ultimate result of losing unity among the elite class is failure to govern. At some point, resources, natural and manmade, become inefficiently utilized for the benefit of the people. The people react with anger and try to replace the politicians they blame. But then the dissatisfaction becomes more widespread, and the political system is threatened.

As we have discussed, America, as a society, cannot survive in an environment lacking moral balance. A single ideology cannot correctly govern a society of different moral positions. Dissonance prevents a balanced morality system from being realized. The complexity of American society today, which includes social and economic stratification, has created a battleground for the right and left to fight for control. Recently, the left has been winning by utilizing the leverage gained by controlling America's intellectual and communications systems.

Value of Tradition

As discussed previously, Edmund Burke was the most well-known proponent of conservatism during the Enlightenment period. He believed that tradition was essential to the stability of modern society. Burke viewed the French Revolution as an absolute catastrophe because its leaders destroyed every practice critical to its existence: the monarchy, the clergy, and the nobility. French society was cast into a political desert lasting 80 years without them. Like it or not, tradition has the vital function of slowing change to an acceptable pace. When a society changes too quickly, there is a damaging impact on its people. That impact is disruptive and causes anxiety.

Tradition exists because it has been a part of human life since man could contemplate his relationship with the universe. His experiences and observation were evaluated, and those seen as essential to his life were retained. For example, religious feelings originally came from the perception that much in life was outside man's control. Religions came into being to interpret and understand the mysteries of life.

Generational Change as a Force

Generational changes constantly impact tradition, but in recent years this has become more focused on the recent generations, Y (millennials, born 1981-1996) and Z (born 1997-2010). Millennials have received outsized attention because they were the first American generation to reach maturity in the Internet age. The internet, computer games, cell phones, and social media have influenced their interaction with the world. The internet age has accelerated human communication tremendously and offered exposure to more information and data than was ever available before. Along with its benefits, there are many dangers, including invasion of privacy, psychological damage, bullying, and exposure to violence. The younger generations will have to reconcile the use of technology with the traditions that hold a society together. Their understanding of technology does not give them an advantage in understanding what lies ahead. They still must think for themselves.

The Problems We Must Solve
The American people must consider moral balance, an evolutionary adaptation developed to increase the odds of surviving in different environments. Moral balance is just as important today as it has ever been. The stakes and problems are higher, so a single ideological approach to governing will not work.

Progress must be driven by decisions that can be reached through negotiations between those with opposing points of view. Those negotiations must be carefully crafted so that change does not occur too quickly. A rapidly changing society is psychologically harmful to human beings. In the same way, a society that experiences too little change causes harm through stagnation. Humans are adaptive creatures, more adaptive than any other species, but our perception of stability in life comes from the balance between old and new. There will always be change because it is embedded in every generation. Still, additional change is placed on a society caused by those in power or forces beyond human control.

The people must hold those in authority accountable for maintaining a stable society.

BIBLIOGRAPHY

Alford, J. R., Funk, C. L., & Hibbing, J. R. *Are political orientations genetically transmitted?* American Political Science Review 99, (2005): 153-167.

Axelrod, Robert and Hamilton, William D. *The Evolution of Cooperation.* Science, New Series, Vol. 211, No. 4489 (March 27, 1981), pp. 1390-1396.

Belloni, Frank P, and Beller, Dennis C. *The Study of Party Factions as Competitive Political Organizations.* The Western Political Quarterly, 29, No. 4 (December 1976): 531-549.

Bernstein, Mary. *Identity Politics.* Annual Review of Sociology, Volume 31, 2005, pp. 47-74.

Burns, James MacGregor *Fire, and Light. How the Enlightenment Transformed the World.* St. Martin's Press, New York, 2013.

Campbell, James E. *Making Sense of a Divided America.* Chapter Title: Ideology and Polarization. Book Title: Polarized. Princeton, New Jersey: Princeton University Press, 2016.

Eagleton, Terry. *The Illusions of Postmodernism.* Oxford, Blackwell Publishers, 1996.

Commager, Henry Steele. Editor. *Lester Ward, and the Welfare State*. New York, Bobbs-Merrill, 1967.

Dean, T. *Evolution and Moral Diversity*. The Baltic International Yearbook of Cognition, Logic, and Communication. 7. doi:10.4148/biyclc.v7i0.1775, 2012.

Edwards, Mickey. *American Tribalism*. Chapter in *The Parties Versus the People*. New Haven, Yale University Press, 2012.

Feuchtwanger, Edgar. *Bismarck*. London, Routledge Press, 1990.

Fraser, Derek. *The evolution of the British welfare state: A history of social policy since the Industrial Revolution*. London, Palgrave McMillan, 1973.

Guilluy, Christophe. *Twilight of the Elites: Prosperity, the Periphery, and the Future of France*. New Haven, Yale University Press. 2019.

Gross, Paul R, Levitt, Norman, and Lewis, Martin W. Eds. *The Flight from Science and Reason*. New York, New York Academy of Sciences, 1996.

Haidt, Jonathan. *The Righteous Mind, Why Good People are Divided by Politics and Religion*. New York: Pantheon Books, 2012.

Harner, Michael J. *Population Pressure and the Social Evolution of Agriculturalists.* Southwestern Journal of Anthropology, Spring, 1970, Vol. 26, No. 1, pp. 67-86.

Hawkins, Stephen, Yudkin, Daniel, Juan-Torres, Miriam, and Dixon, Tim. *Hidden Tribes: A Study of America's Polarized Landscape.* More in Common, 2018.

Jost, J. T., Nosek, B. A., & Gosling, S. D. *Ideology: Its resurgence in social, personality, and political psychology.* Perspectives on Psychological Science, 3, (2008): 126-136, 2008.

Kant, Immanuel. *What is Enlightenment?* Konigsberg, Prussia, September 30, 1784.

Kimball, Roger. *Tenured Radicals: How Politics has Corrupted our Higher Education.* New York, Harper, and Row, 1990.

Kimball, Roger. *The Long March.* San Francisco, Encounter Books, 2000.

Koski, Jessica, Xie, Hongling, and Olson, Ingrid R. *Understanding Social Hierarchies: The Neural and Psychological Foundations of Status Perception.* Soc Neurosci. 2015; 10(5): 527–550. Published online 2015 February 20. doi: 10.1080/17470919.2015.1013223

Langbert, M. *Homogeneity: The Political Affiliations of Elite Liberal Arts College Faculty.* Academic Questions 31:2, 2018.

Lee, P. *The curious life of in loco parentis in American universities.* Higher Education in Review, 8, 65-90. 2011.

Maisel, Sandy. *The Negative Consequences of Uncivil Political Discourse.* Political Science and Politics, V. 45 No. 3 (July) pp. 405-411, 2012.

Marwick, Arthur. *The Sixties.* Oxford, Oxford University Press, 1998.

Mill, John Stuart (1859). *On Liberty.* Batoche Books, Kitchener, Ontario, 2001, Page 13.

Murray, Charles. *Coming Apart: The State of White America, 1960-2010.* New York, Crown Forum, 2012.

Nice, David C. *Polarization in the American Party System.* Presidential Studies Quarterly, Vol. 14, No. 1, Campaign '84: The Contest for National Leadership (Winter), pp. 109-116, 1984.

Paxton, Robert O. *Vichy Lives! – In a way.* The New York Review of Books. Archived from the original on April 14, 2013. Retrieved May 16, 2020.

Riesman, David. *The Lonely Crowd.* New Haven, Yale University Press, 1961.

Robertson, John. *The Enlightenment: A Very Short Introduction*. Oxford, Oxford University Press, 2015.

Ramaswamy, Vivek. *Woke, Inc. Inside Corporate America's Social Justice Scam*. Center Street Publishing, New York, 2021.

Rousseau, Jean Jacques. *Selected Writings: The Social Contract, Discourse on the Origin of Inequality, Discourse on the Arts and Sciences, Discourse on Political Economy*. Translated by D.G.H Cole. Independently published, 2020.

Savio, Mario. *Bodies Upon the Gears Speech*. https://www.youtube.com/watch?v=xz7KLSOJaTE&ab_ch annel=IndridCold. December 2, 1964.

Sanbonmatsu, John. *The Postmodern Prince*. New York, Monthly Review Press, 2004.

Shapiro, Ian. *The Moral Foundations of Politics*. New Haven: Yale University Press, 2003.

Smith, Stephen. *Political Philosophy*. New London, Yale University Press, 2012.

Harvard and Beyond: The University under Siege. Time Magazine April 18, 1969, p.47.

Trattner, Walter I. *From Poor Law to Welfare State*, 6th Edition: A History of Social Welfare in America. Free Press, 2007, p. 15.

Ward, Lester Frank. Forum XX, 1895. Quoted in Harry
Steele Commager's The American Mind: *An Interpretation
of American Thought and Character Since the 1880s—*
New Haven: Yale University Press, 1950, p. 210.

www.ingramcontent.com/pod-product-compliance
Lightning Source LLC
Chambersburg PA
CBHW032053020426
42335CB00011B/323